1 Workbook

Spelling, Punctuation and Grammar

GET IT RIGHT

Frank Danes

Jill Carter

OXFORD UNIVERSITY PRESS

Contents

Introduction — 3

Grammar — 4

1. Nouns — 4
2. Adjectives — 6
   Adjectives in context — 8
3. Verbs: simple present tense and infinitive forms — 10
   Verbs in context — 12
4. Verb tenses: simple past and future — 14
5. Main verbs and auxiliary verbs — 16
6. Subject and object — 18
7. Personal pronouns — 20
8. Possessive pronouns — 22
9. Determiners — 24
10. Prepositions — 26
11. Adverbs — 28
    Adverbs in context — 30
12. Phrases — 32
    Phrases in context — 34
13. Conjunctions — 36
    Conjunctions in context — 38
14. Clauses — 40
    Clauses in context — 42
15. Sentence types — 44
16. Single-clause sentences — 46
17. Multi-clause sentences: Compound — 48
18. Multi-clause sentences: Complex — 50
    Sentences in context — 52
19. Paragraphs — 54
    Paragraphs in context — 56

Punctuation — 58

1. Capital letters — 58
2. Full stops — 60
3. Question marks and exclamation marks — 62
4. Commas — 64
5. Colons and semi-colons — 66
   Colons and semi-colons in context — 68
6. Lists — 70
7. Apostrophes for possession — 72
8. Apostrophes for contraction — 74
9. Direct speech — 76
   Direct speech in context — 78

Spelling — 80

1. Why is spelling important? — 80
2. Vowels and consonants — 81
3. Plurals — 83
4. Silent letters — 84
5. Prefixes — 86
6. Suffixes — 87
7. Commonly confused words — 90
8. How to learn spellings — 92

Glossary — 94

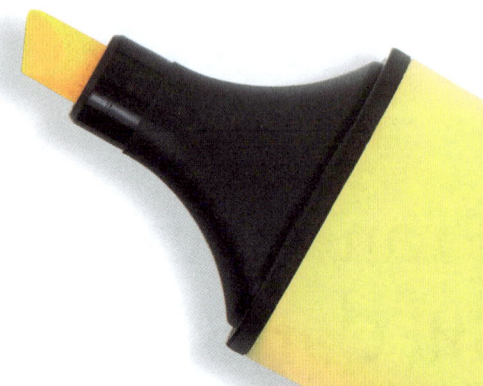

Introduction

How this workbook will help you

This workbook aims to provide you with an accessible introduction to the basics of spelling, punctuation and grammar. The workbook focuses on what you need to know to write fluently and accurately through supportive teaching text and a range of targeted activities.

How this workbook is structured

The workbook is split into three chapters, covering spelling, punctuation and grammar. Each topic in the chapters includes key teaching information and explanation, followed by a range of structured activities to test your understanding.

The workbook also has a clear focus on spelling, punctuation and grammar in context. Selected topics across the workbook feature an 'in context' spread; these spreads include a carefully-selected source text extract and a range of activities that ask you to consider how and why the author has used a particular technique for effect.

Exploring new texts

This workbook introduces you to a range of fiction and non-fiction texts from different historical periods (from the 19th, 20th and 21st centuries), which will help to prepare you for the type of texts you will encounter throughout your English studies.

Which features are included?

The workbook offers a range of varied activities to test your understanding of all the spelling, punctuation and grammar topics, as well as tasks that challenge you to explore the effects of specific grammatical choices in source text extracts. There are spaces to write your answers throughout.

Throughout this workbook, you will find 'Tips' to help support your understanding of difficult concepts, along with a 'Find out more' feature that will direct you to other related topics in the workbook.

For ease of reference, there is also a complete glossary at the end of the workbook that explains all of the relevant spelling, punctuation and grammar terms used throughout the book.

1 Nouns

What are nouns?

Nouns name people, places, ideas or things.

| table | chair | ball | Ben |
| London | Grandma | | |

Geoffrey Chaucer was an author in the Middle Ages.

How do they work?

Nouns can be divided into proper nouns and common nouns.

Proper nouns

Proper nouns are the names of people, places or particular things. They always start with a capital letter.

People's names are proper nouns.

| Zoe Herriot | Stefan Smith | Jake Beckman | Alexander Elder |

The names of places, such as countries, cities, towns, rivers and mountains are also proper nouns.

| India | New York | Birmingham | Nile | Everest |

Days of the week and months of the year are proper nouns.

| Sunday | Wednesday | July | February |

Titles of books, films, newspapers, games and some jobs are proper nouns.

| *The Hobbit* | *Finding Nemo* | *The Times* |
| Monopoly | Prime Minister of the United Kingdom | |

Names of organisations are also proper nouns.

| United Nations | World Health Organisation |
| Oxford University Press | |

Tip

Note that the seasons are not proper nouns, so they don't have a capital letter.

- spring
- summer
- autumn
- winter

Nouns 1

Common nouns

Common nouns name general things rather than particular ones.

These are all common nouns:

girl	boy	man
mug	boots	pizza
door	firefighter	insect
woman	window	car

Common nouns do not have a capital letter unless they are at the start of a sentence.

Tip

Some nouns can be used as both proper nouns and common nouns. When a word is used as a title (like a name) then it should look like a proper noun, and so start with a capital letter.

Noun used as a name, so it starts with a capital letter.

Can I have some money, **Mum**?

My **dad** plays in a band.

Noun used as a common noun, so it has no capital letter.

Activity 1

Underline the proper nouns in the sentences below. The first one has been done for you.

a) Tegan kissed her Aunt Vanessa goodbye and headed to Heathrow Airport.

b) The President of the French Republic waved to his people and climbed aboard the plane.

c) The Prime Minister read the papers gloomily. *The Times* was very critical of the government.

/6

Activity 2

Circle the common nouns in these sentences.

a) The students were very reluctant to let the teachers play volleyball with them.

b) A basket full of crayons, pencils, rulers and stickers fell on Jin's head as she tidied the cupboard.

c) New members should get their passes stamped at the Head's table before heading into the hall.

/14

Activity 3

Fill in the gaps in the text below, using three proper nouns and three common nouns.

Dear _____

Having a lovely time in _____. It is probably the best _____ I have ever had.

The _____ is rather horrible, though, and yesterday I had to tell _____ to send the _____ back because it was disgusting.

/6

Grammar

2 Adjectives

What are adjectives?
Adjectives describe nouns or pronouns.

| soft | hopeful | violent | triumphant |
| rotten | gentle | hilarious | tranquil |

How do they work?
Adjectives give us more information about a noun or pronoun. They often go before a noun.

adjective → The **hungry caterpillar** feasted on the **yellow daffodil**. ← noun
adjective ↗ ↘ noun

Adjectives often follow the verbs **is**, **am**, **are**, **was** and **were**. They describe the noun that is the subject of these verbs.

verb → The crowd **is silent**. ← adjective

Comparative and superlative adjectives

Comparative adjectives compare two things. They often, but not always, end in **–er**.

adjective → Matthew is **tall** but Nimish is **taller**. ← comparative adjective

Superlative adjectives compare more than two things. They often, but not always, end in **–est**.

adjective → Matthew is **tall**, Nimish is **taller** ← comparative adjective
but Sophie is the **tallest**. ← superlative adjective

Some adjectives, often ones with more than three syllables, don't add –er or –est to make the comparative and superlative forms. Instead, they use the words '**more**' and '**most**'.

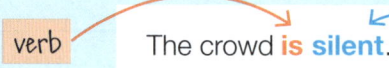

My costume is **ridiculous**. Your costume is **more ridiculous**. His costume is the **most ridiculous**.

↑ comparative adjective   ↑ superlative adjective

Tip
Using more than one adjective at a time can add interest to your writing, see the example below:

> The **foul, wet, clinging** sleet whirled about them.

But don't overdo it, as in this example:

> The **golden, dazzling, awe-inspiring, blazing, astonishing, broiling** sun.

Find out more
See pages 4, 20 and 22 for more about nouns and pronouns.

Adjectives 2

Some adjectives change completely in their comparative and superlative forms. There are examples in the table below.

Basic adjective	Comparative	Superlative
good	better	best
bad	worse	worst

Activity 1

Underline the adjectives in the following text.

Of all the revolting chocolates in the world, our sickly assortment is perhaps the most disgusting. Take, for example, our sticky caramel. Just one tiny taste and your mouth will be immobilised by gluey toffee!

/7

Activity 2

Choose the correct comparative or superlative adjectives in the examples below.

a) These are **gooder / better** bananas. The ones you bought last week were much **worse / badder**.

b) I was even **surpriseder / more surprised** than Ali when I saw who'd emailed. Jake was **most surprised / surprisedest** of all when he saw that she had emailed to apologise.

c) This is the **quickest / most quick** way to the cinema. It is even **more quick / quicker** than going past the park.

/6

Activity 3

Fill in the gaps below with appropriate adjectives.

Astrid was _____ as she eagerly tore open the _____ package. The contents fell out onto the _____ table. They were even more _____ than she had hoped. She whooped excitedly as she studied the _____ instructions.

/5

7

Grammar

Adjectives in context

Extract from 'The Brazilian Cat' by Sir Arthur Conan Doyle, published 1898

In this extract, Marshall King has been locked in an enclosure during the night with a dangerous puma (large wild cat) by his cousin, Everard, who wants him dead. He has managed to seek refuge on top of a cage.

Several times those greenish eyes gleamed at me through the darkness, but never in a fixed stare, and my hopes grew stronger that my presence had been forgotten or ignored. At last the least faint glimmer of light came through the windows – I first dimly saw them as two grey squares upon the black wall, then grey turned to white, and I could see my terrible companion once more. And he, alas, could see me!

It was evident to me at once that he was in a much more dangerous and aggressive mood than when I had seen him last. The cold of the morning had irritated him, and he was hungry as well. With a continual growl he paced swiftly up and down the side of the room which was farthest from my **refuge**, his whiskers bristling angrily, and his tail switching and lashing. As he turned at the corners his savage eyes always looked upwards at me with a dreadful menace. I knew then that he meant to kill me. Yet I found myself even at that moment admiring the **sinuous** grace of the devilish thing, its long, **undulating**, rippling movements, the gloss of its beautiful flanks, the vivid, **palpitating** scarlet of the glistening tongue which hung from the jet-black muzzle. And all the time that deep, threatening growl was rising and rising in an unbroken crescendo. I knew that the crisis was at hand.

refuge place of safety
sinuous having many curves or bends
undulating wavy
palpitating beating rapidly

Activity 1 Understanding the text

a) What time of day is it, according to the second paragraph?

b) How has the arrival of morning affected the puma?

c) Where in the room does the puma pace up and down?

Adjectives in context   2

d) What does the narrator believe the puma intends to do?

----

e) What noise does the puma make?

----

f) Circle the word that is the correct meaning of the word 'grace' in this context.

   elegance   prayer   delay

Activity 2   Exploring the writer's technique

a) What does the adjective 'savage' in the phrase 'savage eyes' imply about the puma?

----

b) Why does the writer use the comparative adjectives 'more dangerous and aggressive' to describe the puma's mood that morning?

----

c) The writer uses the adjectives 'continual' and 'deep, threatening' to describe the puma's growling. How do each of these adjectives help to convey the sound of the puma?

----

d) i. Rewrite the following clause removing the adjectives:
'the vivid, palpitating scarlet of the glistening tongue which hung from the jet-black muzzle'

----

   ii. What is the effect of the clause without the adjectives?

Activity 3   Try it yourself

On a separate piece of paper, write a description of an exotic animal you have seen at a zoo, on holiday or in the media. Think carefully about the adjectives you use. You could use some of the adjectives you have learned from this text.

Grammar

3 Verbs: simple present tense and infinitive forms

What are verbs?

Verbs are sometimes described as doing or being words. Verbs can describe actions.

I **run** through the park, **ride** my bike, then **swim** across the lake. — verbs

Verbs can also describe states of being (rather than physical actions).

I **think** about the problem, then I **imagine** a solution. — verbs

Note that all of these verbs are in the present tense; they describe something that happens now.

How do they work?

Verbs change depending on who is doing the action. The table below shows how the regular verb 'to look' changes.

	Singular	Plural
First person	I **look**	We **look**
Second person	You **look**	You **look**
Third person	He, she, it **looks**	They **look**

A regular verb follows a set pattern, adding different endings, but the basic root of the word stays the same.

An irregular verb changes in a unique way, not following the usual pattern. The table below shows how the irregular verb 'to be' changes.

	Singular	Plural
First person	I **am**	We **are**
Second person	You **are**	You **are**
Third person	He, she, it **is**	They **are**

The infinitive is the basic form of the verb; it has the word 'to' in front of it.

to open   to think   to run   to dream

Tip

Notice the third-person singular form ends –s.

Tip

Notice the first- and third-person singular forms are different to the other forms.

Verbs: simple present tense and infinitive forms 3

Activity 1

Circle the verbs in the sentences below.

a) I mow the lawn and I eat my lunch.

b) Donna wonders whether to turn left or right at the junction.

c) Zahra daydreams and then decides to do her homework.

d) The ice statue melts until the only evidence is a puddle of water.

/9

Activity 2

a) **Complete the sequences of irregular verbs in the table below. Make sure they are all in the present tense.**

	to do	to be	to have
First person	I do	I _____	I have
Second person	You do	You are	You _____
Third person	He, she, it _____	He, she, it _____	He, she, it _____

b) **Choose two of the verbs you have filled in and write two sentences, using one verb in each.**

/7

Activity 3

a) **Circle the verbs in the infinitive form in the sentence below. The first one has been done for you.**

My worst holiday would be (to go) on a long flight, to share a room with

my brother, to visit museums and art galleries and to eat food I don't like.

b) **On a separate piece of paper, complete this sentence using at least three examples of verbs in the infinitive form. Use some of the infinitives below or choose your own.**

to stay   to swim   to play   to buy   to visit   to see   to find   to climb

My perfect holiday would be to --

/7

11

Grammar

Verbs in context

Extract from *One Big Damn Puzzler* by John Harding, published 2006

The following text is taken from the beginning of the novel. The protagonist, William, is being taken ashore for the first time to a very remote island.

As the boat came close to shore William realised that the men had ceased laughing in order to put all their energy into their rowing. He could tell from their strained expressions that the going was getting harder all the time and he deduced that this was because of an **undertow**. The now fairly big waves broke upon a wall of coral
5   that ringed the shore, and bounced back out from it, so that for every ten feet the men rowed the boat was hurled back five. At times it even seemed as if they were thrown back further than they had rowed since the last time, but this must not have been the case as finally they managed to get past the undertow and were riding on the crest of a huge breaker, the oarsmen paddling frantically to steer the craft
10 through a gap in the coral reef, and surfing in on a cauldron of white spray which finally spat the boat out onto a **sickle**-shaped sandy beach. For a moment the men rested over their oars, panting. [...]

As William disembarked into the foaming water swirling around the boat he cursed himself for wearing his **loafers**.

undertow current below the surface of the sea   **loafers** slip-on shoes

sickle a tool with a curved blade

Activity 1   Understanding the text

a) Why do the men rowing the boat stop laughing?

b) What circles the shore of the island?

c) Circle the correct meaning for the word 'surfing' in this context.

   a watersport   browsing the Internet   riding the crest of a wave

d) How do the oarsmen feel when the boat lands?

e) What does William think as he gets out of the boat?

Verbs in context   3

✏ Activity 2   Exploring the writer's technique

a) **i.** Complete the <u>second</u> column below by adding verbs from the extract that describe the movements listed in the first column.

Movements	Verbs	Most powerful verbs, ranking 1 to 3
The movement of the sea		
The movement of the boat		
The movements of the men		

ii. Complete the <u>third</u> column by choosing the three verbs (one from each row) you think are most powerful and rank these from 1–3, with 1 being the most powerful. Explain your decision.

----

b) What does the verb 'deduced' suggest about William?

----

c) What does the verb 'spat' convey in the image at the end of the first paragraph?

----

d) **i.** On a separate piece of paper, rewrite the first paragraph from 'The now fairly big waves…' in the present tense.

   It might start like this:

   > The now fairly big waves break upon a wall of coral that rings the shore, and bounce back out from it, so that for every ten feet the men row, the boat is hurled back five…

   ii. What effect does changing the verbs into the present tense have?

✏ Activity 3   Try it yourself

On a separate piece of paper, write a description of a small boat making its way ashore in a calm sea. Use a range of verbs which convey the ease with which the boat moves. You could also describe the feelings of someone in the boat. You may wish to include some of the vocabulary below:

sailed   cruised   rocked   lulled   dipped   skimmed   glided

13

Grammar

4 Verb tenses: simple past and future

What are verb tenses?

Verb tenses tell us whether something is happening now, has already happened, or will happen in the future.

How do they work?

Verbs change form for different tenses.

Yesterday, you **looked** bored. — past tense
Today, you **look** energetic. — present tense
Tomorrow, you **will look** exhausted. — future

Past tense

Many verbs add **–ed** to make the past tense form.

Present	Past
pack →	pack**ed**
jump →	jump**ed**

> We **packed** all the equipment into the sports cupboard.

Other verbs may change their form completely in the past tense.

Present	Past
buy →	bought
go →	went

> Yesterday, he **bought** new trainers.

Future

The future can be expressed in many different ways. For example, the phrase 'going to' can be used before another verb.

> I am **going to get** my revenge.

Yesterday

Today

Tomorrow

Find out more

There is more about main verbs and auxiliary verbs on page 16.

Verb tenses: simple past and future — 4

The future can also be expressed with the auxiliary verb 'will' in front of the main verb.

I **will make** a pizza.   They **will come** to the party.

Activity 1

Look at the short sentences below. Read each verb below and decide whether it is 'past', 'present' or 'future'. The first one has been done for you.

a) He burbled.   past   b) You will obey me.   ---------------
   He burbles.   ---------------   You obey me.   ---------------
   He will burble.   ---------------   You obeyed me.   ---------------

/5

Activity 2

All of the verbs in the following examples are in the present tense. Change the verbs in each example into the past tense or the future tense.

The first one has been done for you.

a) Angus **swims** strongly through the pool.

   i. past tense: swam
   ii. future tense: will swim

b) Bronwyn **raises** her hockey stick in the air and **charges**.

   i. past tense: --------------- ---------------
   ii. future tense: --------------- ---------------

c) Alasdair **throws** his essay down and **crushes** it under his heel.

   i. past tense: --------------- ---------------
   ii. future tense: --------------- ---------------

/8

Activity 3

Think of a routine you carry out every day. On a separate piece of paper, write three sentences about this routine: one in the past tense, one in the present, and one in the future. For example:

Past: I woke up, got out of bed and looked for my socks.
Present: I wake up, get out of bed and look for my socks.
Future: I will wake up, I will get out of bed and I will look for my socks.

/3

15

Grammar

5 Main verbs and auxiliary verbs

What are main verbs and auxiliary verbs?

A main verb tells us the main action or state or feeling. An auxiliary verb is a 'helping' verb. It comes before the main verb to help express a tense.

auxiliary verb — I **have walked** across a tightrope. — main verb

These are some examples of words that can be used as auxiliary verbs: **am, are, were, does, have, has, was, is, will** and **did**.

How do they work?

Auxiliary verbs

We use the auxiliary verb 'will' to express the future.

auxiliary verb — She **will climb** that mountain. — main verb

We use forms of the verbs 'to be', 'to do' and 'to have' as auxiliary verbs to show questions and more tenses.

auxiliary verb — **Did** you **see** that? — main verb

auxiliary verb — I **am cuddling** the walrus. — main verb

Modal verbs

Modal verbs are also a type of auxiliary verb.

We use modal verbs to express possibility, necessity or the future. These are some examples of modal verbs: **can, could, may, might, should, will, would, shall, must** and **ought to**.

modal verb — Dan **can play** the guitar really well. — main verb

modal verb — I really **ought to revise** for the exam. — main verb

"The main starship engines have failed, Captain!"

"Switch to auxiliary power!"

Remember that the word 'auxiliary' means 'helping' or 'secondary'.

Tip

Remember the different forms of these verbs that can act as auxiliary verbs:

- 'To be': am, are, is, was, were
- 'To do': do, does, did
- 'To have': have, has, had

Main verbs and auxiliary verbs   5

Activity 1

Underline all the main verbs in the sentences below. Then circle all the auxiliary verbs.

a) She was working quietly on her revenge.

b) Sadly, Dad does indeed dance like that.

c) I have bought a skateboard.

d) He did take more than his fair share.

e) Kate will win at least one medal at the games.

/10

Activity 2

a) **Write the correct form of the auxiliary verb 'to be' in the sentences below. Look carefully at the whole sentence to choose the correct tense and use the Tip box on page 16 to help you.**

   i. We _____ training for the marathon last year.

   ii. I can see that you _____ hiding something behind your back.

b) **Write the correct form of the auxiliary verb 'to have' in the sentences below.**

   i. They _____ carried the injured man a long way and are exhausted.

   ii. Today, she _____ confessed to committing the crime.

c) **Write the correct form of the auxiliary verb 'to do' in the sentences below.**

   i. Aneena _____ enjoy watching the skating yesterday.

   ii. I _____ hope you can make the audition.

Find out more

See page 10 for more information about the singular/plural form of verbs.

/6

Activity 3

Write two more sentences, using an auxiliary and a main verb in each. Underline the auxiliary verbs and circle the main verbs.

/4

17

Grammar

6 Subject and object

What is the subject and object?

To find the subject and object in a sentence, you need to look at the verb. The subject is the person, animal or thing that is doing or being the verb. The object is the person, animal or thing that is on the receiving end of the action (having something done to it).

How do they work?

The subject is usually, but not always, near the start of the sentence before the verb. The object usually comes after the verb.

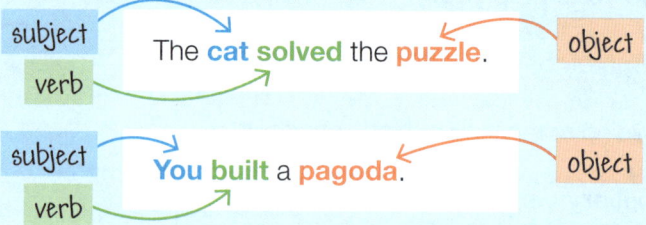

All sentences have a subject and a verb but not all have an object.

For example, this is a full sentence:

This is also a full sentence, but with more detail:

Indirect objects

Some sentences also have an indirect object.

In this example, Simon is the indirect object because he is directly affected after the object.

You can spot an indirect object because it often has a preposition before it.

Tip

To identify the object of a verb, ask:

What is <u>d</u>one, <u>a</u>ffected or <u>c</u>hanged by the verb?

This can be remembered by the mnemonic 'DAC'. A mnemonic is a pattern of letters that will help you remember key words.

Find out more

There is more about prepositions on page 26.

Subject and object 6

Activity 1

Read the sentences and complete the following steps.

- Circle the verb in each sentence
- Underline the subject of the verb in each sentence (the subject can be more than one person)
- Star the object of the verb in each sentence
- Highlight or shade the indirect object in two of the sentences (remember to look for a preposition before it).

a) The girl dug a trench.

b) Afaf lowered the door onto the car's boot.

c) He gutted the fish.

d) Elijah and Elisha smothered the cake with icing.

Tip

Remember that a subject can be more than one word, and can be singular (one) or plural (more than one). For example:

> The **fisherman** and **his son** hauled in the nets.

Both the fisherman and his son are the subject of this sentence.

/15

Activity 2

Add a subject to these sentences.

a) _____ painted a mural in the school hall.

b) _____ thought it looked wonderful.

c) _____ was furious.

d) _____ was featured in the local paper.

/4

Activity 3

Complete these sentences, including an object and an indirect object for the verb. The first one has been done for you.

a) The doctor told <u>me about the good news</u>.

b) Today, Michel is paying _____

c) Under the bridge, Sophie found _____

d) I squeezed _____

/6

19

Grammar

7 Personal pronouns

What are personal pronouns?

Pronouns are words that can be used instead of nouns.

A personal pronoun is used instead of a noun that refers to a person, animal or thing. Some personal pronouns are: **I**, **you**, **she**, **he**, **it**, **we** and **they**.

Tip

'Pro' means 'for', so pronoun means 'for a noun'.

How do they work?

We use pronouns to avoid repeating the noun or nouns. The pronoun 'she' below refers to 'Mel'.

> The thing about Mel is that **she** is always reliable.

The pronoun 'we' refers to 'Dad and I'.

> After Dad and I had been for a walk, **we** painted the shed.

The personal pronouns above are all the subjects of the verbs (they are doing the action of the sentences). If the pronoun is the object of the verb (it is on the receiving end of the action), it may take a different form: **me**, **him**, **her**, **us** and **them**.

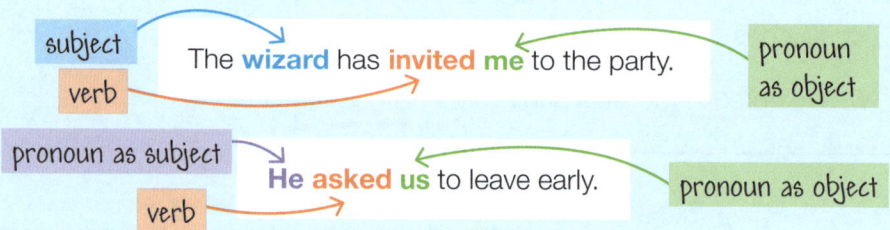

Find out more

See more about subjects and objects on page 18.

The table below is a summary of personal pronouns.

	Singular		Plural	
	Subject	Object	Subject	Object
First person	I	me	we	us
Second person	you	you	you	you
Third person	he, she, it	him, her, it	they	them

Personal pronouns 7

Activity 1

Underline all the pronouns in the sentences. Then draw an arrow to link each pronoun to the noun or nouns it refers to. The first one has been done for you.

a) Peri, will <u>you</u> take the free kick?

b) Talking about Aaron, is he coming too?

c) The hamster thought it should hide.

d) Mary and Martha decided they had finished the chores.

/6

Activity 2

In the sentences below, circle the correct pronoun. The first one has been done for you.

a) I / They / **(He)** gives the crystal to Cho-Je.

b) They grinned when Verity praised **them / they / I**.

c) Mr Atkinson had to tell **she / they / her** to stop talking.

d) **Him / We / Us** hid in the trees when we suspected the pack had picked up our scent.

/3

Activity 3

Complete these sentences, including a personal pronoun in each. The first one has been done for you.

a) If Kamal would like to join the team, <u>ask **him** to come on Saturday</u>.

b) Skyler, would _____
   _____.

c) That man competed in the Paralympic Games and _____
   _____.

d) Mum and _____
   _____.

/3

Tip

Some people get confused about whether to use 'I' or 'me' when linked with another person. For example:

Will and **me** pitched the tent. ✗

This is incorrect. It should be 'I' because it is the subject of the verb. 'Me' would be used when it is the object of the verb. If in doubt, remove the other person and see if it still makes sense, for example:

Me pitched the tent. ✗

I pitched the tent. ✓

Granny gave Kylie and **me** some cake. ✓

Granny gave Kylie and **I** some cake. ✗

Grammar

8 Possessive pronouns

What are possessive pronouns?

Possessive pronouns refer to things that are owned.

The possessive pronouns are: **mine**, **yours**, **hers**, **his**, **its**, **ours** and **theirs**.

How do they work?

Possessive pronouns always link back to what has already been referred to, but they give an idea of ownership.

For example, imagine these people arguing over a chocolate:

That hat's **mine**! Give it back!

Oh, don't be so possessive.

"That chocolate is **mine**." — meaning 'belongs to me'
"It is not **yours**!" — meaning 'belonging to you'
"Maybe it is **his**." — meaning 'belongs to him'
"Or **hers**?" — meaning 'belongs to her'
"No, it is **ours**." — meaning 'belongs to us'
"I think it is **theirs**." — meaning 'belongs to them'

The relationship between personal pronouns and possessive pronouns looks like this:

Personal pronouns		Possessive pronouns
I	me	mine
you		yours
she	her	hers
he	him	his
it		its
we	us	ours
they	them	theirs

Tip

Be careful using the possessive pronoun 'its'. It never has an apostrophe, to avoid confusion with the contraction for 'it is' or 'it has'.

The government has completed **its** master plan.

Possessive pronouns 8

Activity 1

Circle the possessive pronouns in the email below. There are six in total. The first one has been done for you.

Hello Grandpa!

We are having a wonderful time. The rooms in the hotel are great, or at least, (mine) is. Alice keeps complaining about hers because she says it's full of geckos, but the island is theirs after all so she should put up with it. David's room looks out over the sea. Yours does too. It's such a pity you couldn't come.

We have made the resort ours by bagging the best places by the pool every day; the hotel says it's not its policy to allow us to be 'selfish' but I don't know what they mean.

Wish you were here!

Love Rose

/5

Activity 2

Complete the following sentences by adding the correct possessive pronoun.

a) Charlotte thought of it, so the idea was _____ and not Huang's.

b) I picked up Nathan's keys by mistake. I didn't realise they were _____.

c) We gave out all the packed lunches, saw that Michelle and Toby didn't have one, and concluded that these spare lunches must be _____.

/3

Activity 3

You are giving out prizes at a children's party but you are not sure who has won what. Your friend is helping you out.

Complete this activity by filling in your friend's speech bubbles with a possessive pronoun. The first example has been done for you.

Is this prize Dan's? — Yes, it's <u>his</u>.

And is this one Jasmine's? — Yes, it's _____.

So is this Yuan and Honey's? — Yes, it's _____.

Which makes this one for you and me? — Yes, it's _____.

/3

23

Grammar

9 Determiners

What are determiners?

A determiner comes before a noun and gives more information about it, such as which one it is, how many there are, where it is and whose it is.

These words can all be used as determiners: **the**, **a**, **an**, **my**, **your**, **five**, **those**, **that**, **whose**, **enough**, **more**, **less**, **each**, **any** and **some**.

How does it work?

The most common determiners are these words: **the**, **a** and **an**.

The determiner **the** (also called the 'definite article') refers to something specific that is known.

> **the** shop in **the** village

The determiners **a** and **an** (also called the 'indefinite articles') refer to something more general that is non-specific.

> **a** café in **an** arcade

Possessive determiners

Possessives determiners show ownership. Some are names with a possessive apostrophe.

> **Yana's** racket was stolen. — *possessive determiner*

The following possessive determiners also show ownership: **my**, **your**, **his**, **her**, **its**, **our** or **their**.

> I know what **their** problem is. — *possessive determiner*

Quantifying determiners

Quantifying determiners tell us quantity or number: **all**, **many**, **these**, **those**, **fifty**, **some**, **less**, **fewer**, **no** or **enough**.

> **forty-seven** sailors   **some** ice creams   **fewer** fans — *quantifying determiners*

Find out more

See page 72 for more information about possessive apostrophes.

Determiners 9

Demonstrative determiners

Demonstrative determiners show us (demonstrate) which one by saying whether it is near or far: **this**, **that**, **those** and **these**.

> this wolf   that sofa   those clowns   these games

Tip

The word 'them' is a pronoun and should never be used as a determiner. For example:

> **Them** shoes ✗
> **Those** shoes ✓

Activity 1

Underline the determiners in the sentences below. There are two in each sentence. The first one has been done for you.

a) <u>A</u> newt and <u>an</u> aardvark have escaped.

b) There are some shoes in the shop.

c) Tatiana's advice is more effective than Lucy's medicine.

d) Let every student choose a piece of fruit.

e) Each day brings a new challenge.

/8

Activity 2

Add a different possessive determiner to each of the sentences below. The first one has been done for you.

a) <u>Their</u> team won last year.

b) _____ plan has failed again.

c) _____ spacesuit was ruined.

d) _____ cat is crazy.

e) _____ joke was the best.

/4

Activity 3

Some words can be used as determiners or another word class. Look at the underlined words in each sentence below. Tick if they are used as a determiner. Add a cross if they are not.

a) Would you like <u>some</u> chips? ☐

b) I already have <u>some</u>. ☐

c) <u>Either</u> pizza will be fine. ☐

d) I said <u>no</u>. ☐

e) <u>These</u> boots are made for walking. ☐

f) I can't believe <u>that</u>. ☐

Tip

Remember that a determiner always comes before a noun or a noun and its adjectives.

/6

25

Grammar

10 Prepositions

What are prepositions?

A preposition usually comes before a noun, pronoun or noun phrase (a group of words that has a noun as its key word) and links it to other words in the sentence. Prepositions can tell you about position, direction, timing or another type of link or relationship.

These words can be used as prepositions: **with**, **since**, **from**, **to**, **opposite**, **between**, **under**, **over**, **through** or **of**.

How does it work?

The prefix **pre-** means 'before,' so the preposition usually (but not always) goes *before* the noun, pronoun, or noun and its adjectives.

Some prepositions show direction or position: **upon**, **outside**, **inside**, **in**, **into**, **above**, **across**, **beneath**, **below**, **among**, **beyond**, **on**, **of**, **around**, **opposite**, **towards**, **under**, **by** and **near**.

preposition — A troll stood **opposite** the **cottage**. — noun

Some prepositions show timing: **since**, **while**, **as**, **before**, **during**, **after**, **for**, **until**, **throughout**.

preposition — He had been waiting **since** the *early* morning. — noun
adjective

Other prepositions show a link or relationship between things. Note that some are more than one word: **against**, **by**, **with**, **without**, **of**, **about**, **through**, **including**, **from**, **except for** and **according to**.

preposition — He waited **for** the **fisherman**. — noun

Find out more

See page 4 for more information about nouns.

Tip

The most common preposition is 'of', for example:

The coat **of** many colours

The opposite **of** brave

The owner **of** the dragons

Prepositions — 10

Activity 1

Underline all the prepositions in the paragraph below. There are ten in total.

> She led them into the tunnel. There was barely a metre between them as they sloshed through the water. Icy droplets dripped from the ceiling and seeped into their clothes. They walked in silence until they spotted a dim light. All of them, except for Clive, felt a chill of fear.

/10

Activity 2

Fill in the spaces with appropriate prepositions. The first one has been done for you.

a) The mice ran <u>towards</u> the princess's feet and <u>under</u> the dresser.

b) Toby drilled _____ the wall and _____ the water pipe.

c) Chelsea played _____ Liverpool.

d) Make sure you finish your homework _____ you go out.

e) He leaned _____ the wall.

f) Rebecca put the letter _____ the envelope.

g) We haven't got any eggs so you'll have to make the cake _____ them.

h) Don't make a phone call _____ you're driving the car!

/8

Activity 3

You are setting out on a quest. Write a short paragraph to describe your preparations, including at least three prepositions. Use the starter sentence to begin.

I stuffed my food rations **into** my rucksack. _____

_____

_____

_____

_____

_____

/3

11 Adverbs

What are adverbs?

Adverbs describe verbs, adjectives or other adverbs. They often, but not always, end **–ly**.

| hungrily | noisily | greedily | revoltingly | sadly |
| surprisingly | strangely | unfortunately | definitely | |

Tip

Remember that both **ad**verbs and **ad**jectives add description!

How do they work?

Adverbs often describe verbs.

adverb — Moon Chi **greedily gobbled** his lunch. — verb

Adverbs can also describe adjectives.

adverb — The bed was **unpleasantly hard**. — adjective

Adverbs can also describe other adverbs.

Leo moved away from the snake **very slowly**. — adverb / adverb

He knew **instinctively** that something was under the bed.

The adverb 'very' is called an intensifier because it intensifies, or emphasises, another adjective or adverb.

Other intensifying adverbs include: **really, extremely, totally, terribly, completely, so** and **too**.

Adverbs of time and frequency tell us when something is taking place and how often it happens. These include: **tomorrow, later, earlier, soon, often, sometimes** and **rarely**.

I **rarely** see my old friends from primary school.

Some adverbs can act as a cohesive device, which means that the adverb can link a sentence back to the previous one. (They are sometimes known as 'connectives'.) These include: **soon, later, finally, firstly, next, afterwards, therefore, however, also, furthermore, eventually, nevertheless** and **overall**.

Veterinary surgeons train for many years. **However**, they are well paid once they qualify.

Adverbs 11

Activity 1

Underline the adverb in each sentence below. Then decide whether the adverb is describing a verb or an adjective and circle the correct answer. The first example has been done for you.

a) Theresa was <u>very</u> happy when she became a professional singer.

   This adverb describes **a verb / (an adjective)**.

b) Liam felt bitterly cold that first night at camp.

   This adverb describes **a verb / an adjective**.

c) He was surprisingly unprepared even after revising all night.

   This adverb describes **a verb / an adjective**.

d) Jenna gingerly manoeuvred the starship out of space dock.

   This adverb describes **a verb / an adjective**.

e) Yasmin carefully unpacked her suitcase.

   This adverb describes **a verb / an adjective**.

f) Michael cheerfully sang the terrible song with his little brother.

   This adverb describes **a verb / an adjective**.

/10

Activity 2

Underline the adverbs in the sentences below. The first one has been done for you.

a) The gale blew <u>sharply</u> into her frozen face.

b) Lukas ran noisily downstairs and tore open his presents feverishly.

c) Clara carefully applied her make-up and silently opened the front door.

d) I sent it to you yesterday.

e) Ahmed was really sorry to miss the match.

/6

Activity 3

Each of the following sentences needs an adverb to make it more interesting. Add a suitable adverb in the space provided.

a) Aaliyah swam _____, knowing she was on the point of winning.

b) Rhys approached the monster _____, knowing it was likely to wake up.

c) Janina _____ contemplated the glittering ballroom.

d) We will go to the planet Neptune _____.

e) _____, she had enjoyed the book.

/5

29

Grammar

Adverbs in context

Extract from 'Homes of the London Poor' by Octavia Hill, published 1883

This extract is from an article by Octavia Hill, a woman who campaigned for better housing and green spaces and helped to establish the National Trust.

First, then, as to places to sit in. These should be very near the homes of the poor, and might be really very small, so that they were pretty and bright, but they ought to be well distributed and **abundant**. The most easily available places would be our disused churchyards. I have myself no fear that the holy dead, or those who loved
5   them, would mind the living sharing in some small degree their quiet. There is a small, square, green churchyard in Drury Lane, and even the sight of its fresh bright **verdure** through the railings is a blessing; but if the gates could be opened on a hot summer evening, and seats placed there for the people, I am sure the **dwellers** about Drury Lane would be all the better for it. Again, round St. Giles's Church
10   there is space for many seats under the trees. The number of people to be seen in Leicester Square (since the garden was thrown open to the public) show how glad people are of a seat in the open air. But Leicester Square shows us also another thing: such places must be made bright, pretty, and neat—a small place which is not so becomes painfully dreary, and it is quite **curious** to notice how little one feels shut in
15   when the barriers are lovely, or contain beautiful things which the eye can rest on.

abundant plentiful
verdure greenery
dwellers residents
curious interesting

Activity 1 — Understanding the text

a) Where does Octavia Hill believe pleasant open spaces should be located?

b) Circle the correct meaning of the word 'degree' in this context:

   an academic qualification   a measure of temperature   an amount

c) What kind of place does Hill suggest could be used for this purpose?

d) What does Hill say these places should be like and why?

Adverbs in context 11

✏ Activity 2 Exploring the writer's technique

a) The writer begins this paragraph with the adverbs, 'First, then'. How does this help to introduce her argument?

....

....

b) Identify the three adverbs that act as intensifiers in the second sentence. Why do you think the writer uses two intensifiers together when she does? What effect does this have?

....

....

c) In the third sentence, Hill suggests that disused churchyards are the 'most easily available places' for people to use. How does the adverb 'easily' further her argument?

....

....

....

d) In the final sentence, Hill uses the phrase 'painfully dreary'. What effect does the adverb 'painfully' have in this phrase?

....

....

....

✏ Activity 3 Try it yourself

On a separate piece of paper, draft an email to your local council asking them to improve an open space you know of. Explain the value of a pleasant open space and how it can make you feel. Use adverbs to help convey your ideas.

For example, you could include intensifiers such as:

very   **extremely**   **definitely**   **undeniably**   **certainly**

and adverbs that add detail to your verbs, such as:

playing **merrily**   walking **contentedly**   relaxing **calmly**

You could begin like this:

> Dear Sir/Madam,
>
> Our local park is potentially a stunning open space for people to enjoy...

31

Grammar

12 Phrases

What are phrases?

Phrases are usually groups of words that work as units. Most phrases do not have a verb, so they are not full sentences.

These are all phrases:

in front of the palace	behind the tree
a jar of honey	as quickly as possible

How do they work?

All phrases have a key word, which is known as the 'headword'. It is the most important word in the phrase. The other words in the phrase support (give more detail about) the headword.

There are many different types of phrases.

A noun phrase acts as a noun and has a noun as its headword.

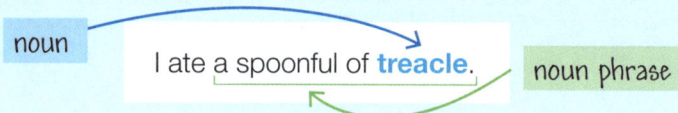

An adjective phrase acts as an adjective and has an adjective as its headword.

An adverb phrase acts as an adverb and has an adverb as its headword.

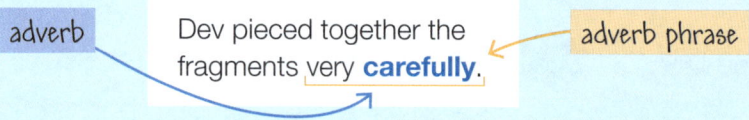

A prepositional phrase acts as a preposition and has a preposition as its headword.

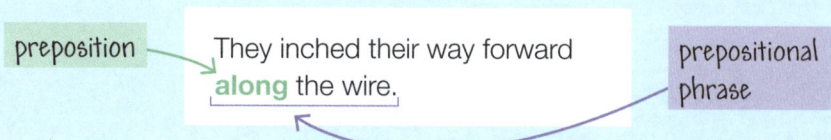

Find out more

If a phrase contains a verb, we call it a clause. See page 40 for more on clauses.

Find out more

There is more about nouns on page 4, adjectives on page 6, adverbs on page 28 and prepositions on page 26.

Phrases 12

Activity 1

a) **Circle the headword in the underlined noun phrase.**

She has many sports <u>trophies</u>.

b) **Circle the headword in the underlined adjective phrase.**

Matthew is very <u>enthusiastic</u> about his new trombone.

c) **Circle the headword in the underlined prepositional phrase.**

The plane circled <u>above</u> the airport before landing.

d) **Circle the headword in the underlined adverb phrase.**

Please gather up your belongings as <u>quickly</u> as you can.

/4

Tip

Remember a noun phrase works like a noun; an adjective phrase works like an adjective; an adverb phrase works like an adverb; a prepositional phrase works like a preposition.

Activity 2

Read the phrases below. Circle the headword in each and tick to show what type of phrase it is. The first one has been done for you.

	Noun phrase	Adjective phrase	Adverb phrase	Prepositional phrase
(through) the tunnel				✓
that miserable giant				
really quickly				
painfully slow				
the purple-haired boy				
opposite the bench				

/10

Activity 3

Expand the following noun, adjective, adverb or preposition into phrases. The first one has been done for you.

a) Write a noun phrase using the noun *marmalade* as your headword.

<u>A jar of marmalade</u>

b) Write a noun phrase using the noun *milk* as your headword.

----

c) Write an adjective phrase using the adjective *excited* as your headword.

----

d) Write an adverb phrase using the adverb *soon* as your headword.

----

e) Write a prepositional phrase using the preposition *against* as your headword.

/4

Grammar

Phrases in context

Extract from 'Save our children from the horrors of school sport' by John Harris, *The Independent*, 1 March 2000

In this extract from his article, John Harris describes his efforts to succeed at forward rolls.

> In anticipation of writing two simple words, I am already the victim of creeping anxiety. A film of sweat begins to coat my palms, my head is swimming with visions of ogre-like teachers and I feel a deep sense of shame. Anyway: forward rolls… there, I've done it.
>
> 5   When I was six or thereabouts, my inability to move myself a couple of feet, via the strange **expedient** of turning my body through 360 degrees, was a major source of trauma. My teachers quite reasonably believed that such a handicap would turn me into an unemployed **vagrant**, so I was forced to spend several months correcting it.
>
> Just short of my seventh birthday, I cracked it. I now proudly include the ability to do
> 10 forward rolls on my **curriculum vitae**.

expedient means of achieving something

vagrant person without a settled home or work

curriculum vitae (CV) brief account of someone's education and work experience, which is used when applying for a job

Activity 1 — Understanding the text

a) Circle the correct meaning of the word 'film' in this context:

- to record moving images
- a fine coating
- a movie

b) How does the writer claim to be feeling at the beginning of this extract?

c) How long did the writer spend learning to do forward rolls properly?

d) How old was the writer when he 'cracked it'?

Phrases in context   12

✏ Activity 2 — Exploring the writer's technique

a) Identify the headword from each noun phrase in the table below. Comment on the effect of the writer's use of noun phrases. Consider what the additional words add to the headword before you comment on effect.

Noun phrase	Headword	Effect of noun phrase
creeping anxiety		
a film of sweat		
ogre-like teachers		
an unemployed vagrant		

b) Choose a phrase that shows that the writer is exaggerating. Remember that a phrase does not include a verb. Explain your choice.

----

c) What prepositional phrase does the writer use to describe his age when he succeeded in doing forward rolls? Why is this phrase more interesting than, for example, *When I was six*?

✏ Activity 3 — Try it yourself

On a separate piece of paper, write a short article for a magazine about a time when you succeeded at something you found difficult. Use noun phrases to help exaggerate your feelings. You may wish to include some of the ideas below:

- wave of rising terror
- sense of increasing panic
- overriding fear of failure
- steely determination to succeed
- amazing pride in my abilities

Grammar

13 Conjunctions

What are conjunctions?

Conjunctions are joining words. They can link words, phrases or clauses.

Conjunctions can also be called 'connectives'.

How do they work?

There are two types of conjunctions:

- coordinating conjunctions
- subordinating conjunctions.

Coordinating conjunctions

Coordinating conjunctions join two parts of a sentence that are of equal weight (they are both main clauses).

Coordinating conjunctions include: **and**, **or**, **nor**, **but**, **yet**, **so** and **for**.

> coordinating conjunction → You like jam **but** I like marmalade, ← clauses of equal importance

Subordinating conjunctions

A subordinating conjunction joins a less important part of the sentence (subordinate clause) to the most important part of the sentence (main clause).

Subordinating conjunctions include: **because**, **although**, **though**, **while**, **for**, **before**, **whether**, **since**, **so**, **after**, **until**, **if**, **as**, **even**, **though** and **whereas**.

> You may go home now **although** we haven't finished our studies today.
> (main clause) (subordinating conjunction) (subordinate clause)

All of these subordinating conjunctions (except 'for') can be used at the start of a sentence.

> **Because** I'm a lovely person, I will let you off this time.
> (subordinating conjunction)

Find out more

See page 40 for more about clauses.

Tip

Some people prefer not to start a sentence with a conjunction – especially 'and' or 'but'. However, it is not ungrammatical to do so and can produce interesting results. For example:

> **And** that was the end of that.

Conjunctions 13

Activity 1

Underline all the coordinating conjunctions in the paragraph below. The first one has been done for you.

Mobile phones are not allowed in lessons <u>and</u> tablets are also banned. Anyone who disobeys this rule will be punished, so you know what to expect. You will not be allowed to leave at 3.30 on Friday, nor will you be given a break that day. I have always enforced this punishment, but I might be less strict if you give me names of pupils who have broken this rule. I can't promise to be lenient, yet I will consider being fair.

/4

Activity 2

Use a subordinating conjunction to join the two parts of the sentences below.

a) We shall hunt down the dragon _____ it tries to hide itself.

b) I shall rule the world _____ I have had my afternoon nap.

c) You should take your umbrella _____ it probably isn't going to rain.

d) They were not frightened _____ they were holding hands.

e) You will invite your cousin to your party _____ you like him or not!

/5

Activity 3

Read the statements below and tick whether they are true or false.

Statements	True	False
a) A conjunction can also be called a connective.		
b) A conjunction can only link clauses together.		
c) The following words are subordinating conjunctions: although, because, whereas.		
d) A subordinating conjunction links clauses of equal importance.		
e) The following words are coordinating conjunctions: and, but, or.		

/5

37

Grammar

Conjunctions in context

Extract from *Etta and Otto and Russell and James* by Emma Hooper, published 2015

In this extract from the novel, Etta, who is 83, has decided to walk across Canada to see the sea.

She stopped for food in the rest-stop café in Holdfast. They had changed the tables and chairs since she was last there, with Alma. Less colour, cleaner. Nobody noticed her come into town and nobody noticed her leave, except for the waitress and the boy at the till.

5 After eating three cabbage rolls, two pieces of white bread with butter and one slice of rhubarb pie, and paying for them, Etta left with ten sachets of ketchup and eight of green relish tucked into her coat pocket. Relish was vegetable and sugar and ketchup was fruit and sugar and either could see you through if you needed them to.

It was just starting to get dark when, little by little, the crops began to thin and the
10 ground began to turn sandy and then to sand completely. And then, just as the sun sat down below the stretching orange of the horizon, Etta stopped walking; having made her way right up to a lake, right up to the water, just far enough away from the push of the waves to stay dry. She knew, of course, that she would encounter obstacles of smaller water before she was through to Halifax. She'd heard Ontario
15 was full of them. But she didn't expect anything quite so soon. She sat down on the sand, a few metres from the wet edge. It felt good to sit.

Activity 1 — Understanding the text

a) What had changed at the café when Etta returned there?

b) What does Etta take away with her from the café and why?

c) Circle the correct meaning of 'relish' in this context: to enjoy   a strong-tasting sauce or pickle

d) What time of day is it when Etta stops walking?

e) What prevents Etta from walking any further?

Conjunctions in context 13

✏ Activity 2 — Exploring the writer's technique

a) The first paragraph includes coordinating and subordinating conjunctions. Identify one example of each.

Coordinating conjunction	Subordinating conjunction

b) The writer begins the second paragraph with a subordinating conjunction and a subordinate clause. How does this add impact to the sentence?

---

c) In the third paragraph the writer begins one sentence with 'And then'. A student reading this paragraph said:

> Starting this sentence with a conjunction emphasises the sudden change in Etta's journey.

What do you think is the effect of starting a sentence with 'But' on line 15 of the extract?

---

d) Throughout the text the writer frequently uses the conjunction 'and'. What effect does this have on the reader? Tick the interpretations you agree with most and explain why.

It helps to convey the way in which Etta is experiencing a lot of new things. ☐

It reflects the endlessness of the journey she has started. ☐

It suggests the way in which she keeps moving onwards. ☐

✏ Activity 3 — Try it yourself

On a separate piece of paper, write a short account about part of a journey you have experienced or imagined. Include three sentences that start with the following:

And   But   a subordinating conjunction

39

14 Clauses

What is a clause?

A clause is a group of words that work together as a unit with a verb as its headword.

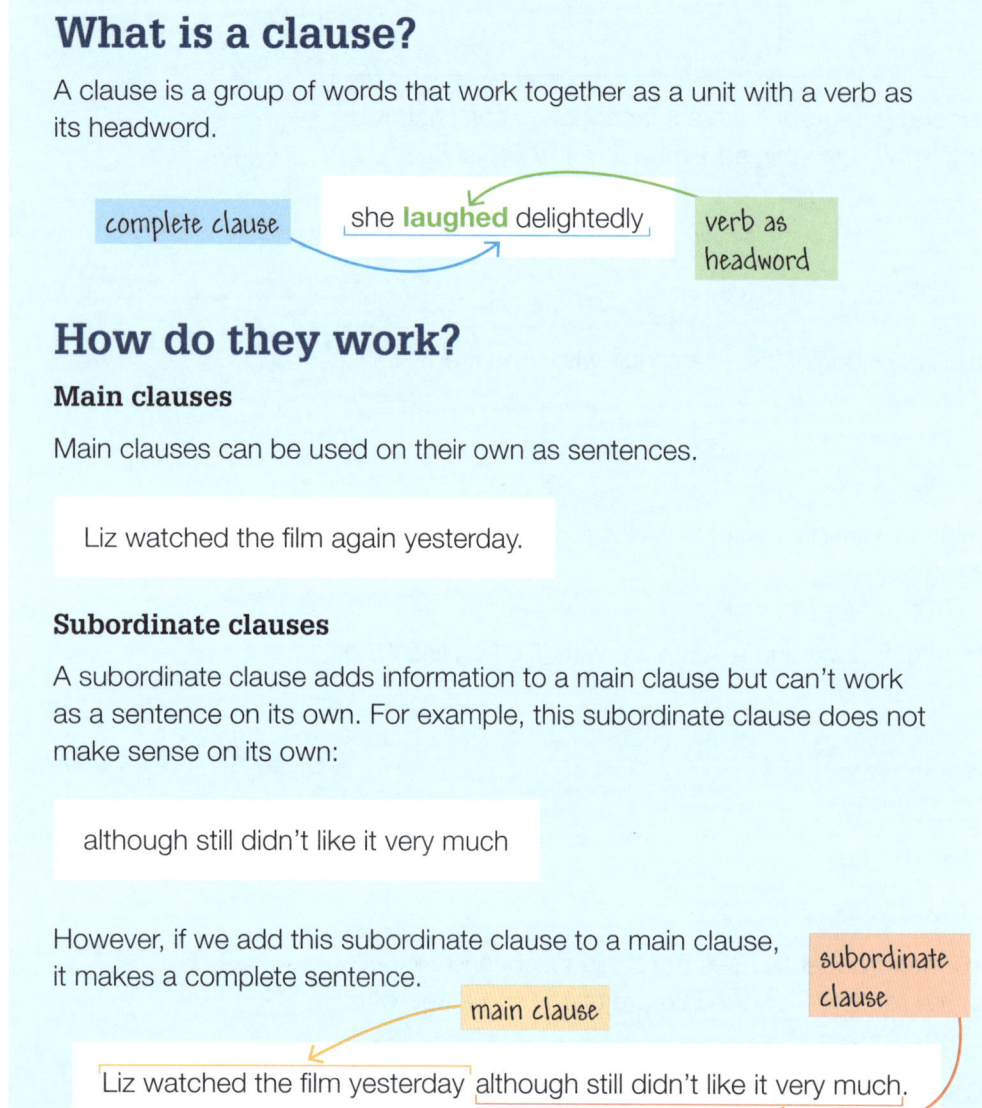

How do they work?

Main clauses

Main clauses can be used on their own as sentences.

Liz watched the film again yesterday.

Subordinate clauses

A subordinate clause adds information to a main clause but can't work as a sentence on its own. For example, this subordinate clause does not make sense on its own:

although still didn't like it very much

However, if we add this subordinate clause to a main clause, it makes a complete sentence.

Liz watched the film yesterday although still didn't like it very much.

We can recognise subordinate clauses because they start with subordinating conjunctions, such as: **because**, **although**, **though**, **while**, **for**, **before**, **whether**, **since**, **so**, **after**, **until**, **if**, **as**, **even though** and **whereas**.

A subordinate clause can be at the start of a sentence:

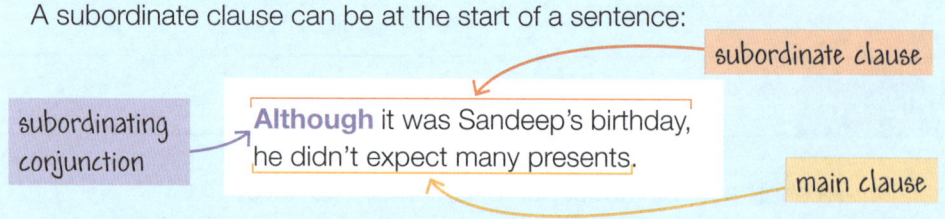

Find out more

See page 36 for more about conjunctions.

Clauses 14

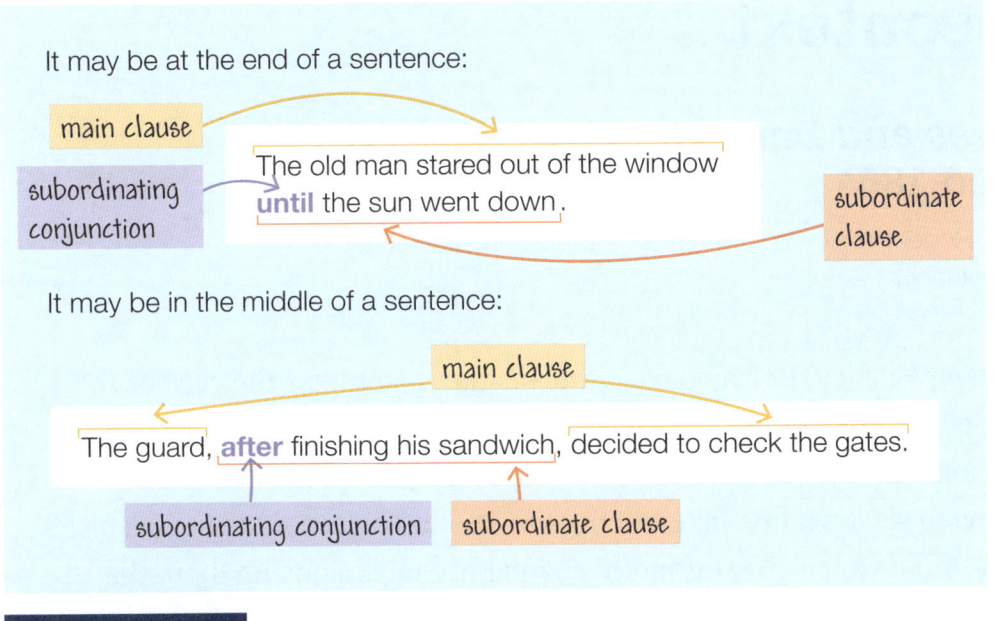

Tip

Note that a subordinate clause in the middle of a sentence is marked off from the rest of the sentence with two commas: one before and one after the subordinate clause.

Activity 1

Read the sentences below carefully and decide how many clauses are in each. The first one has been done for you.

a) Everyone was very hungry. `1`

b) He will be furious if you betray him. ☐

c) Han stayed with us for the whole weekend. ☐

d) Kaylee scored a goal just before the referee blew the whistle. ☐

e) I carried the food and Jason brought the equipment. ☐

f) Three goblins strolled across the school playing field. ☐

/5

Activity 2

In the sentences below, underline the subordinate clauses and circle the subordinating conjunctions. The first one has been done for you.

a) The picnic was cancelled (because) it was raining.

b) Although it was chilly, they bought ice creams from the van.

c) Unless you apologise, Martha won't take you to the restaurant.

d) The pizza spun wildly through the air before landing on the floor.

e) Let's make some popcorn while we wait for the film.

f) Until you lost your voice, I didn't realise how much you talk.

/10

Activity 3

On separate paper, write a sentence containing a main clause and a subordinate clause. Highlight the main clause and underline the subordinate clause. Circle the subordinating conjunction.

/3

41

Grammar

Clauses in context

Extract from *Wives and Daughters* by Elizabeth Gaskell, published 1864

In this extract from the novel, Roger Hamley, a young man with a keen interest in the natural world, walks home for lunch.

> She did not see Roger Hamley returning from the meadows, nor hear the click of the little white gate. He had been out **dredging** in ponds and ditches, and had his wet sling-net, with its imprisoned treasures of nastiness, over his shoulder. He was coming home to lunch, having always a fine midday appetite, though he pretended to despise
> 5 the meal in theory. But he knew that his mother liked his companionship then; she depended much upon her luncheon, and was seldom downstairs and visible to her family much before the time. So he overcame his theory, for the sake of his mother, and had his reward in the hearty **relish** with which he kept her company in eating.
>
> He did not see Molly as he crossed the terrace-walk on his way homewards. He
> 10 had gone about twenty yards on the small wood-path at right angles to the terrace, when, looking among the grass and wild plants under the trees, he spied out one which was rare, one which he had been long wishing to find in flower, and saw it at last, with those bright keen eyes of his. Down went his net, skilfully twisted so as to retain its contents, while it lay amid the **herbage**, and he himself went with light
> 15 and well-planted footsteps in search of the treasure.
>
> **dredging** dragging a net along the bottom of an area of water
>
> **relish** enjoyment
>
> **herbage** plants and greenery

Activity 1 — Understanding the text

a) What has Roger Hamley been doing?

b) Find two reasons why Roger goes home for lunch.

c) What does Roger consider to be 'treasure'?

d) How does Roger treat the natural world around him?

Clauses in context   14

✏️ Activity 2 — Exploring the writer's technique

a) Circle the coordinating conjunction in the first sentence of the text. What kind of clauses does this conjunction link?

---

b) Re-read the following sentence: 'He was coming home to lunch, having always a fine midday appetite, though he pretended to despise the meal in theory'.

   i. Underline the main clause.

   ii. Identify the two subordinate clauses and explain in your own words the extra information they provide about Roger.

---

c) i. Rewrite the first two sentences using simple sentences that contain only one clause in each.

---

   ii. What do you notice about how different the text is now?

---

d) In the clause, 'and he himself went with light and well-planted footsteps in search of the treasure', what impression is the reader given of Roger's approach to nature?

✏️ Activity 3 — Try it yourself

On a separate piece of paper, describe an interest or hobby you have using some longer sentences that contain main and subordinate clauses. Use these subordinate clauses to add interesting details to your writing.

Remember that words such as the ones below can introduce a subordinate clause:

| because | although | while | before | since | until | if | whereas |

43

15 Sentence types

What are sentences?

Sentences are groups of words that express complete ideas. They usually have a verb and form a statement, question, command or exclamation.

How do they work?

In writing, every sentence:

- starts with a capital letter
- consists of one or more clause
- always has at least one verb
- usually has a subject
- ends with a full stop (.), a question mark (?) or an exclamation mark (!). These punctuation marks show that the sentence is complete. If you are reading aloud, they are usually where you take a breath.

Sentences are used for different purposes:

- To make a statement (tell you something):

  The fish swims contentedly in its bowl.

- To ask a question:

  Would you like to ride on a camel with me?

- To show an exclamation (express emotion such as surprise or enthusiasm):

  What a fantastic present!

- To give a command (tell you to do something). Commands normally start with a verb:

  Go to the back of the queue.

Don't miss the bus!

> **Tip**
>
> Note that an exclamation does not always need to include a verb or subject.

Sentence types 15

Activity 1

Add a capital letter and full stop to each sentence in the table below. Then tick whether it is a statement or a command.

Sentence	Statement	Command
a) the horse lifted its head and listened with interest		
b) come with me to the beach		
c) clara consulted the map and then turned the ignition key		
d) mathematics had never held much interest for Mohun and he found himself daydreaming as Mr Brown droned on		
e) choose your favourite meal and eat it quickly		

/10

Activity 2

Decide whether the sentences below are questions, exclamations, commands or statements and tick the appropriate box. The first one has been done for you.

	Statement	Question	Exclamation	Command
a) Step away from the cookie jar.				✔
b) How fabulous you look!				
c) Close your eyes and imagine the scene.				
d) The wizards were taking a quick nap.				
e) Have you got the exact change for the admission fee?				
f) I hope you have kept your promise.				
g) Take my advice and leave now.				

/6

Activity 3

In the text below, two people are having a conversation. Add the appropriate punctuation mark at the end of each sentence. The first one has been done for you.

a) Jo asked, "Are you looking forward to going to the stadium with your dad tomorrow _?_ "

b) Harry shrugged, "Not particularly __"

c) Jo became irritated. "Well, why not __"

d) Harry said shortly, "Because we always lose __"

e) Jo lost her temper. "You are so ungrateful __ Your father works all hours so he can take you to the football __ Think about that __"

f) Harry, unfussed, muttered under his breath, "Oh, here we go again __"

/7

Grammar

16 Single-clause sentences

What are single-clause sentences?
Single-clause sentences have just one main clause. They are also known as simple sentences.

How do they work?
Single-clause sentences have only one subject and one verb. They may or may not have an object.

subject — The **cat ate**. — verb

subject — The **cat ate the fish**. — verb / object

Here are some more examples of single-clause sentences:

subject — **Donna read** enthusiastically. — verb

subject — **Donna read her book** enthusiastically. — verb / object

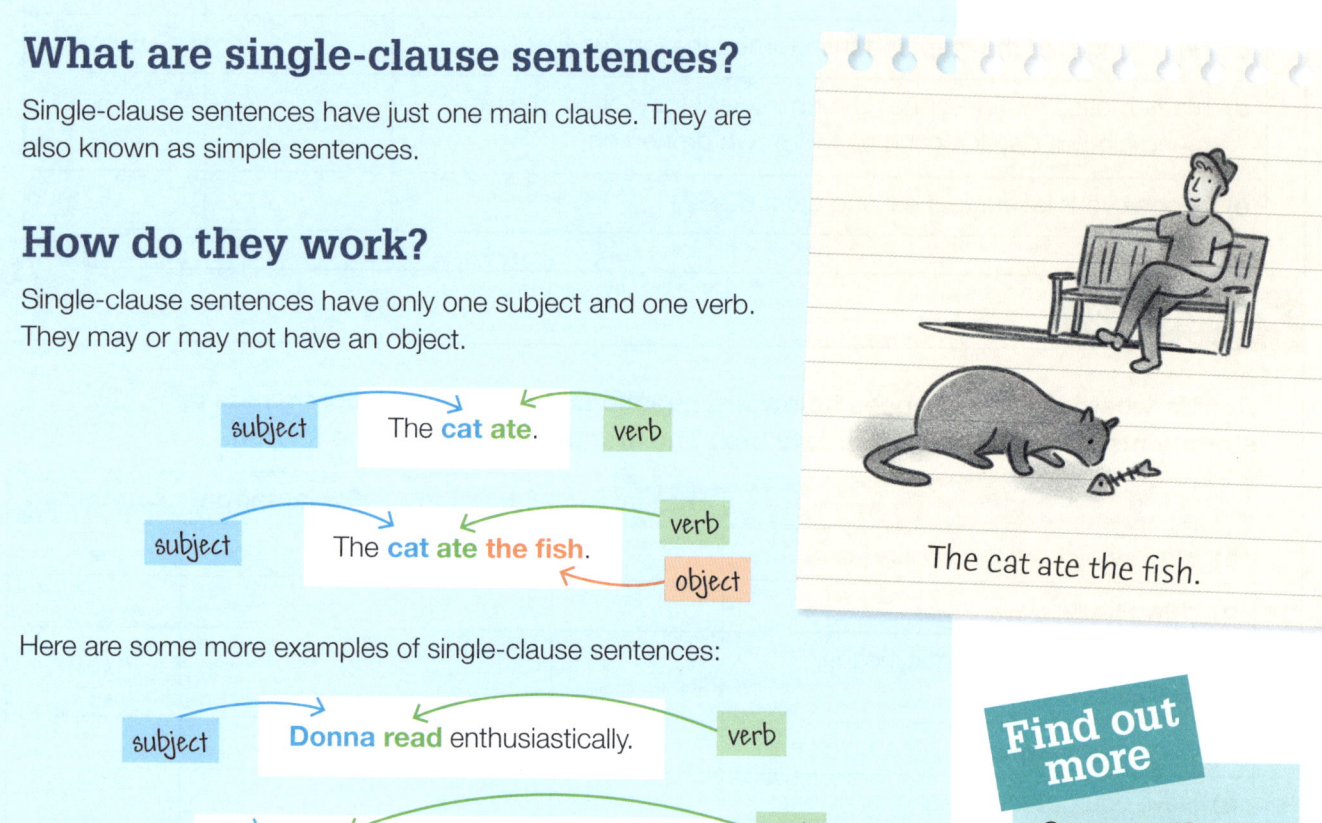

The cat ate the fish.

Find out more
See page 40 for more about clauses.

Activity 1

In each of the texts below there are three single-clause sentences. Add the missing capital letters and punctuation to mark the start and end of the sentences.

a) sujata was feeling unwell she had a temperature she slipped under her duvet

b) the lion sat on the antelope the antelope wriggled furiously the lion looked away

c) i opened my wallet it was empty i was very surprised

/6

Single-clause sentences 16

Activity 2

Underline the four single-clause sentences in this text. Remember that a single-clause sentence has just one clause.

Gorillas are apes. They are closely related to human beings and live in groups called troops. Troops contain one adult male, several females and their offspring. A male gorilla is called a silverback. Gorillas are highly intelligent. Some gorillas in captivity have even been taught to use sign language and they can use four or five words consecutively, although some scientists doubt if this is true.

Tip

Remember that a single-clause sentence must include only one main clause, however this doesn't mean that they are always short in length, as they can include additional phrases.

/4

Activity 3

Write three single-clause sentences. Underline all the verbs, circle the subjects and highlight or star the objects.

You can use some vocabulary from the groups below or you can choose your own.

Subjects	Verbs	Objects
bat	took	fruit
Ivan	texted	bite
Sophia	chewed	rhubarb
cow	built	message
I	grew	grass
we	ate	Dad

a) ....

b) ....

c) ....

/9

Grammar

17 Multi-clause sentences: Compound

What are multi-clause sentences?

Multi-clause sentences are made up of more than one clause.

Some multi-clause sentences contain two or more main clauses. These are also known as compound sentences.

The main clauses in compound sentences are joined together by coordinating conjunctions, such as **and, but, or, nor** and **yet**.

How do they work?

Here are two single-clause sentences, each made up of one clause:

The cat sat on the mat. It thought about life.

Here is a multi-clause sentence, made up of two main clauses joined by a coordinating conjunction.

first main clause — The cat sat on the mat **and** thought about life. — coordinating conjunction
second main clause

Here are more multi-clause sentences, using different coordinating conjunctions:

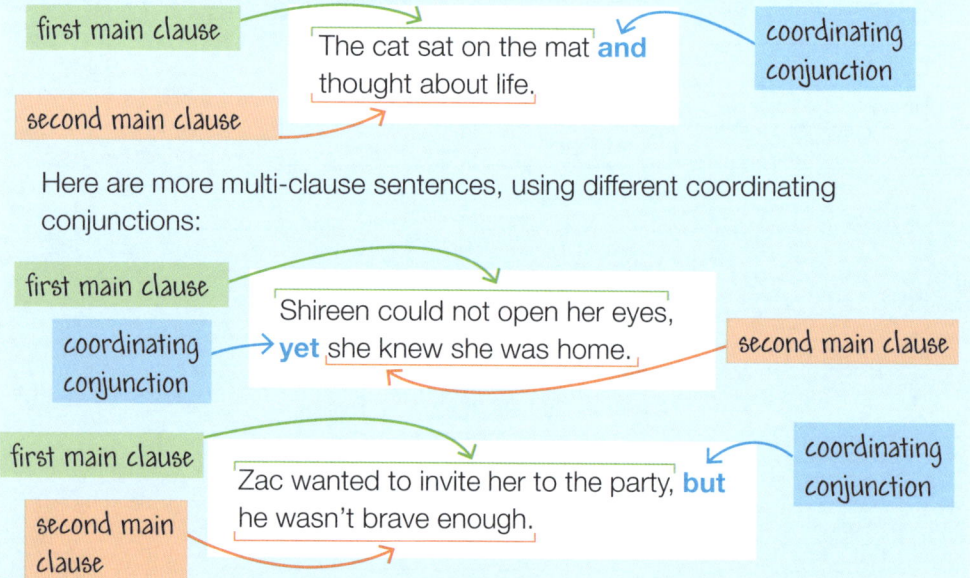

Find out more

See page 40 for more about clauses. See page 36 for more about conjunctions.

Tip

Notice that in a multi-clause sentence we sometimes leave out the subject in the second clause.

The cat sat on the mat and ~~the cat~~ thought about life.

Multi-clause sentences: Compound 17

✏️ Activity 1

Rewrite the pairs of single-clause sentences below, changing each pair into one multi-clause sentence. You will need to:

- add a coordinating conjunction such as 'and', 'or', 'but', using each one only once
- decide whether to keep or drop the subject (noun or pronoun) in the second clause
- change the punctuation as necessary.

The first one has been done for you.

a) Mickey threw his phone down. He stamped upstairs.

   Mickey threw his phone down and stamped upstairs.

b) She entered the code word again. It was no use.

-----

c) Ahmed could paint the fence blue. He could paint the fence red.

-----

d) Polly liked her new school. She liked her new lime green uniform.

/6

✏️ Activity 2

a) Underline the one multi-clause sentence in the paragraph below.

b) Circle the coordinating conjunction.

> Dr Seuss wrote many books. One of his most successful books was *The Cat in the Hat*. It was based on a list of first words for children. Dr Seuss included all the list's words in his book and created one of the most popular children's books of all time.

/2

✏️ Activity 3

On separate paper, write three multi-clause sentences of your own using a coordinating conjunction (such as: and, but, or, nor, so, for, yet) to join your equally important clauses together.

You might like to write about yourself, where you live, your favourite pastime, your favourite food or a person you admire.

/6

18 Multi-clause sentences: Complex

What are complex sentences?

Some multi-clause sentences contain one main clause and at least one subordinate clause. These are also known as complex sentences.

The main clause and subordinate clause in complex sentences are joined together by subordinating conjunctions, such as: **after**, **although**, **because**, **before**, **if**, **since**, **as**, **unless**, **when**, **whether**, **until**, **though** and **whereas**.

Some subordinating conjunctions are more than one word, such as: **as soon as**, **so that**, **as long as**, **in order to** and **provided that**.

How do they work?

Main clauses can make sense on their own. Remember a clause is a group of words that work together as a unit with a verb as its headword.

> The ship's maiden voyage had to be postponed

A subordinate clause does not make sense on its own.

> as the forecast was so bad.

However, when put together, the subordinate clause supports the main clause, adding more information to it.

main clause
> The ship's maiden voyage had to be postponed **as** the forecast was so bad.
subordinating conjunction — *subordinate clause*

In some multi-clause sentences, the subordinate clause comes before the main clause. This can make the information in the subordinate clause seem more important.

subordinate clause
> **If** you arrive late at school, you must report to reception.
subordinating conjunction — *main clause*

Find out more

See page 40 for more about clauses. See page 36 for more about conjunctions.

Betty could see the boat in the distance, although it didn't seem to be getting any nearer.

Multi-clause sentences: Complex 18

Activity 1

Look at the clauses in the table below. Decide whether each is a main clause or a subordinate clause and tick the correct box. The first one has been done for you.

	Main clause	Subordinate clause
you can't see that film at the cinema	✔	
provided that we have enough time		
since you're both still far too young		
Victoria drank her coffee carefully		
in order to avoid her sensitive tooth		

/4

Activity 2

Complete the sentences below by writing a subordinate clause after the main clause.

Remember that the subordinate clause should start with a subordinating conjunction. The first one has been done for you.

a) You need to put the car in the garage <u>since it might rain this afternoon</u>.

b) Do please invite your friends round to tea _____

c) Of course you can go to the bowling alley tomorrow _____

d) Adjoa loved that film _____

/3

Activity 3

A subordinate clause can go at the beginning, in the middle or at the end of a sentence. Write a subordinate clause in the gap in each of these sentences.

a) When Grandpa comes to stay, _____, we will make him welcome.

b) _____, do remember to tell him to wipe his feet.

c) You can certainly go out to play soccer _____

/3

Grammar

Sentences in context

Extract from *What I Was* by Meg Rosoff, published 2008

In the following extract from the novel the narrator, Hilary, has sneaked out of boarding school to spend more time with his new friend Finn.

It began to hail. We hunched our shoulders and huddled into our coats, me in my regulation school topcoat, Finn in a canvas jacket that didn't look very warm, neither of us with gloves. ==Exhaling white puffs of condensation, we hurried along, our footsteps hollow in the narrow cobblestone streets.== It was dark and cold and
5 almost everyone was indoors. On each side of the narrow street, cottages leant in towards us, leaking murmuring voices and small slivers of golden light. I felt like a moth, drawn to the cosy rooms beyond the shutters and curtains, rooms crammed with figurines and ugly suites of furniture where red-faced men and women watched the telly and mongrel collies snored. Smoke from a hundred coal fires
10 poured out of chimneys and swirled around us in the frigid air. […]

It wasn't until we were out of town that he spoke. 'Shouldn't you be at school?'

I stopped, eyes wide. 'That's rich coming from you.'

He kept walking, and I skipped to catch up. 'I've given up. Nothing left to learn.'

He turned to gauge my expression, and one side of his mouth twitched up in amusement.

Activity 1 — Understanding the text

a) What is the weather like as the boys walk through the town?

b) Where are most of the town's residents?

c) Where does the narrator feel he would like to be?

d) How does the narrator feel about school?

e) Circle the correct meaning of the word 'gauge' in this context:

the distance between rails on a track   a measuring instrument   to measure

Sentences in context **18**

Activity 2 — Exploring the writer's technique

a) What effect does the single-clause sentence have at the beginning of this text?

----

b) Underline an example of a compound sentence in the text. Explain how the ideas in the sentence you have found are of equal importance.

----

c) Re-read the multi-clause sentence highlighted in yellow in the extract on page 52.

   i. Circle the main clause of the sentence.

   ii. Rewrite this sentence in two other ways by moving the clauses around. Explain which of the combinations you prefer.

----

d) Re-read the sentence beginning 'I felt like a moth…'.

   i. What kind of sentence is this?

----

   ii. What effect does the longer subordinate clause have on the reader?

----

e) What kind of sentences does the writer use in the dialogue between Hilary and Finn? Why do you think the writer does this?

Activity 3 — Try it yourself

On a separate piece of paper, write about a walk you have taken with a friend, using a range of single and multi-clause sentences for effect.

19 Paragraphs

What are paragraphs?

A paragraph is a sentence or group of sentences on one idea that forms a distinct section in a piece of writing. Paragraphs help to break up a text to make it easier to understand. What you are reading now is a paragraph.

How do they work?

The rule is **one paragraph: one idea**.

In a text, a new paragraph should begin every time there is a significant change, such as:

- a change of time
- a change of place
- a new event
- a new topic
- a new person speaking.

A new paragraph is usually punctuated by an indent in the first line or by leaving a line space.

Paragraphs can be very long. Charles Dickens sometimes wrote two-page paragraphs. Paragraphs can also be very short – just one short sentence.

Varying the length of paragraphs can make writing more interesting. A very short paragraph within longer paragraphs can have a dramatic effect and make it stand out.

Tip

The best way to learn how to write paragraphs is to read widely: novels, newspapers, magazines, biographies. If you read a lot, you absorb the rules of using paragraphs and get a natural feel for when and how you should use them.

Activity 1

The following extract about emperor penguins needs to be divided into three paragraphs: one about the location, one about the penguins, and one about the predators.

Your task is to mark where the paragraphs should go. Mark each paragraph break in the text with the symbol '||' and write NP (short for 'New Paragraph') in the margin.

Remember to use the rule *one paragraph: one idea*.

Antarctica, in the southern hemisphere, is one of the most hostile environments in the world. Winds can blow at 90 miles per hour and the temperature can fall to −40 degrees. The emperor penguin is one of the most beautiful of all the penguins and is native to Antarctica. An emperor penguin can stand up to 130 cm in height and has a beautifully streamlined body that is adapted for swimming. Orcas – killer whales – will attack penguins in the water, as will leopard seals. Other predators are two species of birds: the south polar skua and the giant petrel.

/3

Activity 2

The following extract needs laying out in paragraphs. Write it out again, starting a new paragraph every time:

- there is a change of speaker
- there is a change of subject.

> "I don't like the new cinema," said Trina. "What's wrong with it?" asked Sharon, who knew what was coming next. "It's ugly and it looks like a giant shed dumped in the middle of a field." Sharon started gathering her things together. It was time to go to work. "Also," Trina complained, "there's the green issue. They've spoiled the countryside." "Yes, dear, whatever you say," Sharon said, struggling into her coat. She cared as much as anyone about the environment but sometimes she wished Trina would talk about something else.

/5

Grammar

Paragraphs in context

Extract from *American Shaolin* by Matthew Polly, published 2007

The following extract is taken from the autobiography by Matthew Polly, who trained to become a fighter at the Shaolin Temple in China and represented the Temple at the Zhengszhou tournament, a major Chinese kickboxing competition.

As I stepped onto the platform, the realisation that he'd dropped me to the **canvas**, kicked me twice, and tossed me off the **leitai** in less than thirty seconds settled over me like a heavy weight. With absolute certainty I knew he was too good for me. There was no way I was going to win. As we faced each other again, I could hear
5 these words bouncing around inside my skull: *Pride. Too good. Face. Coach Cheng. Pride. Deqing. He's too good. Pride. You're fighting for pride now.*

So I started to dance. I shuffled. I backpedalled. I circled around the ring using my longer arms and legs to keep him out of range. It wasn't **Ali**, but I was dancing. Shuffle. Punch. Backpedal. Shuffle. Kick. I had generalship of the ring, if only for
10 a brief moment. In my head I was moving faster than in fact I was, but still I held the Champ off for the rest of the round. I'd closed the scoring gap but not enough: 20–10 was my best guess.

The five referees lifted their cards. They were all black for my opponent.

I'd lost the round but salvaged my pride.

15 But I wasn't thinking about that when I returned to my metal chair where Coach Cheng and Deqing were waiting for me between rounds. As I sat down, I didn't believe I would ever be able to stand up again.

canvas a strong, coarse, unbleached cloth **Ali** Mohammed Ali, a famous boxer
leitai fighting platform

Activity 1 Understanding the text

a) What is the writer's situation at this point in the fight?

b) What does Polly tell himself he is fighting for now?

c) What does Polly do to try to gain some control of the fight?

Paragraphs in context **19**

  d) Circle the correct meaning of the word 'shuffle' in this context:

  to move without lifting the feet   to rearrange or mix up

  e) How does Polly feel once he sits down?

Activity 2 — Exploring the writer's technique

a) Complete the table below to summarise what each of the five paragraphs is about.

Paragraph 1	
Paragraph 2	
Paragraph 3	
Paragraph 4	
Paragraph 5	

b) Look again at paragraphs 1 and 2. Why do you think the writer starts a new paragraph when he does?

----

c) The writer uses two very short paragraphs. What effect do these paragraphs have on the reader?

Activity 3 — Try it yourself

On a separate piece of paper, write an account of a time when you did something challenging. Use paragraphs to show how events developed. Use a variety of paragraph lengths, including at least one dramatic one-sentence or two-sentence paragraph.

Punctuation

1 Capital letters

What are capital letters?

There are two types of letters:

- small (lower case) letters, such as: a b c d e f g
- capital (upper case) letters, such as: A B C D E F G.

How do they work?

Capital letters are used for many different reasons.

- For the first letter in a sentence:

  This is a photograph.

- For the first-person pronoun 'I':

  Alem and **I** went to school together.

- For months of the year or days of the week:

  April   **J**uly   **T**hursday

- For times of the year that many people consider special, such as:

  Christmas **D**ay   **D**iwali   **R**amadan   **P**assover

- For the names of particular people, places and buildings:

  David   **Y**ork   **C**hina   **E**iffel **T**ower   **A**tlantic **O**cean

- For the title of books, films, plays, newspapers, magazines, poems, and songs:

  Fantastic Mr Fox   *Black Panther*   *War Horse*

- For brand names, such as retailers and products:

  Nike   **A**ldi   **I**kea   **A**didas   **G**ap   **C**ineworld   **A**mazon

Tip

Common nouns, such as mum, dad or granny, are all lower case, unless they are used as a name in which case they take an initial capital, like a proper noun.

> She asked her **m**um if she had seen her bag.
>
> "Have you seen my bag, **M**um?"

Find out more

See page 20 for more about personal pronouns.

Tip

In titles, less important words, such as **a**, **an**, **and**, **the**, and **of**, are usually lower case.

Capital letters 1

Activity 1

There are three pairs of sentences in the table below. Which of each pair uses capital letters correctly? Tick either 'correct' or 'incorrect' for each sentence.

Sentence	Correct	Incorrect
a) i. i have no idea why I'm expected to go to the Shops tomorrow.		
ii. I have no idea why I'm expected to go to the shops tomorrow.		
b) i. Yosef politely accepted Aunt Sarah's invitation to lunch on Sunday.		
ii. Yosef politely accepted aunt sarah's invitation to lunch on Sunday.		
c) i. It was Hot in the robot costume and jon couldn't wait to take it Off.		
ii. It was hot in the robot costume and Jon couldn't wait to take it off.		

/6

Activity 2

Add capital letters to the sentences below. The first one has been done for you.

a) I walked down Larkin Street and went into the newsagent to buy a copy of *The Observer*.

b) hale knew that the gang planned to meet in brighton on sunday 1 march, the first day of spring.

c) winston smith is the hero of george orwell's novel *nineteen eighty-four*.

d) zoe quite liked going to mars and certainly found jupiter much more interesting than her boring old home town, barchester.

e) my father has noisy taste in music: his favourite band is blondie and their hit song 'atomic'.

f) "please mum, can I have another twenty quid? everyone else's mum has paid up."

/5

Activity 3

An address uses capital letters, as it refers to a very specific place. For example:

76 Totter's Lane
Shoreditch
London
W1A 4WW

On a separate piece of paper, write your own address using capital letters correctly.

/4

Punctuation

2 Full stops

What is a full stop?

A full stop is a punctuation mark used to mark the end of a sentence.

How do they work?

Full stops show that a sentence is complete and finished. When a text is read aloud, a full stop represents a significant pause. It is sometimes where the reader might take a breath.

Traditionally, full stops have also been used to show that a word or words have been shortened or abbreviated.

> Rev. (short for Reverend)
>
> a.m. (short for *ante meridiem*, meaning 'before noon')
>
> p.m. (short for *post meridiem*, meaning 'after noon')
>
> e.g. (short for the Latin *exempli gratia*, meaning 'for example')
>
> etc. (short for the Latin *et cetera*, meaning 'and other things')

The use of full stops to show an abbreviation is becoming less common. We often see abbreviations without full stops.

> GCSE (short for General Certificate of Secondary Education)
>
> MP (short for Member of Parliament)
>
> USA (short for the United States of America)
>
> BBC (short for the British Broadcasting Corporation)

Abbreviations that use the first letter of each word in a name or term that then make another word are called 'acronyms'.

> NASA   LOL   GIF

Find out more

Some people use commas incorrectly instead of full stops. See page 64 for more about this error, called 'comma splicing'.

Jess had lots of plans for his trip to Greece **e.g.** sightseeing, visiting friends and trying the local food.

Full stops 2

✏ Activity 1

Read the following statements about full stops in the table below. Tick whether they are true or false.

Statement	True	False
a) A full stop shows where to pause in a sentence.		
b) A full stop is used to show the end of a sentence.		
c) A full stop must always be used to show an abbreviation.		
d) Full stops are sometimes used to show abbreviations.		
e) An acronym always needs full stops.		

/5

✏ Activity 2

There are two sentences in each of the examples below, but they are missing the correct punctuation. Add the missing full stop and capital letter in each example. The first one has been done for you.

a) Salman looked carefully at the grim-faced men standing before him. **A**ny moment now, one of them was going to try to sell him something he didn't want.

b) The maths exercise was child's play to Sophia she had taken hundreds of similar tests in the last six months.

c) Jamie contemplated the food without enthusiasm as usual, his brother hadn't bothered to cook it properly.

d) He was close to tears he had been learning the spells for hours now but could not remember a single one of them.

e) She threw the cricket ball hard it sailed over the fence and broke the greenhouse's window.

/8

✏ Activity 3

Write these abbreviations out in full.

a) Rev. ----

b) No. ----

c) Prof. ----

/3

61

Punctuation

3 Question marks and exclamation marks

What are question marks and exclamation marks?

Question marks and exclamation marks are punctuation marks that are usually placed at the end of a sentence. They indicate that the sentence is a question or an exclamation.

How do they work?

A question mark comes at the end of a sentence that asks a direct question.

> Does this question mark look like the hook of a coat hanger?
> Have you tidied your room?

An exclamation mark comes at the end of a sentence that shows a sense of drama or strong emotion, such as anger, surprise, shock, delight or horror.

> What a disaster this is!
> You've bought me that football shirt I wanted!

It can also show a warning.

> Beware – giant hamsters!
> Don't go too close to the edge!
> Stop!
> Keep out!

If you use a question mark or an exclamation mark at the end of the sentence, the next sentence must start with a capital letter.

> Are you going to take responsibility for your actions?
> Don't just shrug your shoulders, answer the question.
>
> Don't touch it! Now you've burned yourself.

Tip

Exclamation marks are effective however more than one exclamation mark at a time is unnecessary and is considered informal English.

Find out more

There is more about different sentence types on page 44.

Question marks and exclamation marks 3

Activity 1

Read the sentences below. Add a question mark to the questions and a full stop to the statements.

a) Did you know that you have four miles of tubing in your stomach

b) I don't think that's actually possible

c) Can you imagine what she must be feeling after her victory

d) You seem to have eaten all the biscuits

e) Have you eaten all the biscuits

f) Why are you that strange green colour

/6

Activity 2

Read the following statements about exclamation marks and question marks. Tick whether they are true or false.

Statement	True	False
a) An exclamation always ends with a question mark.		
b) An exclamation can be a warning.		
c) A question mark can come at the start of a sentence.		
d) An exclamation mark can show strong emotion.		
e) A question mark is always followed by a full stop.		
f) You cannot have too many exclamation marks.		

/6

Activity 3

The sentences below are missing their final punctuation marks. Decide what type of sentence they are and add an appropriate punctuation mark.

a) Get away from the cliff edge

b) Why is it that old people don't understand young people

c) The three children slept peacefully through the night

d) How many times did Julius Caesar refuse to be crowned as king

e) What a great party

f) Eggs, flour and milk, when mixed together properly, can make a delicious cake

/6

Punctuation

4 Commas

What are commas?

A comma is used to separate information. It can separate:

- items in a list
- clauses
- direct speech from information about the speaker.

When reading aloud, a comma indicates a short pause.

How do they work?

Commas separate items in a list when those items are short and simple.

> Please ensure that you bring the following equipment: a tent, a groundsheet, sleeping bags and food.

We don't usually include a comma before the 'and' and the final item in a list unless it is necessary to make sense.

> We ate soup, pasta, beef and carrots, and rhubarb and custard.

A comma can also separate clauses in a multi-clause sentence.

> Sarah ran down the street, until she caught up with Daniel.

main clause — Sarah ran down the street,
subordinate clause — until she caught up with Daniel,
comma

A comma can also separate direct speech from information about a speaker.

> "We're going to be late," shouted Dad.

Comma splicing

Beware of using commas when full stops or another form of punctuation such as a semi-colon should be used instead. This is called comma splicing. Commas should *not* separate full sentences.

Tip

A comma placed before the final item in a list, before the word 'and', is known as the 'Oxford comma' or 'serial comma'.

Find out more

There is more about direct speech and its punctuation on page 76. There is more about semi-colons on page 66.

Commas 4

Activity 1

There are three pairs of sentences in the table below. Which of them use commas correctly? Tick either 'correct' or 'incorrect' for each sentence.

Pairs of sentences	Correct	Incorrect
a) i. Maya wanted to visit Egypt, France, Spain and Australia.		
ii. Maya wanted to visit, Egypt, France, Spain, and Austalia.		
b) i. "No one can blame me," he laughed.		
ii. "No one can blame me" he, laughed.		
c) i. The light was fading, fast so we headed home.		
ii. The light was fading fast, so we headed home.		

/6

Activity 2

Insert a comma in each of the sentences below, to separate out the clauses. The first one has been done for you.

a) Dorothy devoured the orange, tossing the skin aside after eating the last piece.

b) I think you should go home and change even though the others disagree.

c) Although no reason was given the wedding invitation was withdrawn.

d) As it was her birthday Zoe slept in till nine o'clock.

e) Let's take some money although I doubt we'll need it.

f) You are asking for trouble going back to your home town.

/5

Activity 3

The paragraph below has been written by a student who is comma splicing. Decide where full stops should be used instead of commas and mark them in the paragraph.

> He reached the bottom of the cliff, when he looked up, he could barely see the top, the clouds were so low that they hung half way down the sheer wall, the seagulls wheeled and cried above him, he inspected the rock face for hand and toe holds, there were none, it was going to be an almost impossible climb.

Tip

Try reading the paragraph aloud. You can often tell where you need a full stop by when you need to take a breath, or when a point in the text finishes.

/6

Punctuation

5 Colons and semi-colons

What are colons and semi-colons?

A colon looks like this **:**

A colon can be used to introduce a list, examples or explanations.

> He thought her everything a prime minister should be: brave, determined and strong.

colon

A semi-colon looks like this **;**

A semi-colon links together two main clauses that are of equal importance but suggest a contrast or are closely related.

semi-colon

> She downloaded the song on to her iPod; satisfied, she ran off to find Sunil.

A semi-colon can also be used to separate longer, detailed items in a list that needs clearer division than just with commas.

When reading aloud, the colon and semi-colon both show a pause.

How do they work?

Colons

A colon is used to show that something is to follow. It can be used in many things:

- lists

> In the village shop, you will find: milk, eggs, newspapers, bread, cheese and Mr Magister the shopkeeper.

- direct speech or quotations

> She said: "Are you sure time travel is that dangerous?"

- explanations.

> Rory got the job: the manager was his wife.

Find out more

See page 70 for more about the use of colons and semi-colons in lists.

Find out more

There is no need for a capital letter after a colon or semi-colon unless it is a proper noun. There is more about proper nouns on page 4.

Colons and semi-colons 5

Semi-colons

A semi-colon is used to join two main clauses together that suggest a contrast, or that are very closely related. Both the main clauses could stand alone as sentences. The benefit of the semi-colon is that it shows a stronger relationship between the clauses than a full stop would.

> We are going to the festival tomorrow; I bet it rains.

semi-colon separates two main clauses and shows a strong relationship between them

Activity 1

Use a semi-colon to join these sentences together. The first one has been done for you.

a) Victoria laced up her bowling shoes reluctantly; she didn't like the noisy, crowded bowling alley on Saturday nights.

b) Mike wanted to go to Bristol Zoo very much. He was much less interested in the proposal to visit the Science Museum.

c) She pulled on her running gear and trainers. She was out of the door before her aunt had noticed that she'd gone.

d) She realised she'd left something behind as soon as she left the house. Her memory was definitely getting worse.

/3

Activity 2

Add a colon in the correct place in the following examples.

a) He replied "It's only dangerous if you don't take the proper precautions."

b) These, then, were the reasons for her delight her mother's kindness and the gift of two tickets to the Broadway musical.

c) Moon Chi approached the new headteacher's door with terror the new headteacher was his father.

/3

Activity 3

Add either a semi-colon or colon in the square brackets in the sentences below.

a) Hugh asked [ ] "Are you really going to marry him?"

b) Saskia pulled open the curtains [ ] the sun had risen with dazzling beauty.

c) Don't forget to bring these items on the plane [ ] sunglasses, a book, your phone, your passport and the tickets.

/3

Punctuation

Colon and semi-colons in context

Extract from *The Secret History* by Donna Tartt, published 1993

In this extract the narrator, Richard Papen, looks back on his childhood.

> In fact, when I think about my real childhood I am unable to recall much about it at all except a sad jumble of objects: the sneakers I wore year-round; coloring books and comics from the supermarket; little of interest, little of beauty. I was quiet, tall for my age, **prone to** freckles. I didn't have many friends but whether this was due to choice or **circumstance** I do not now know. I did well in school, it seems, but not exceptionally well; I liked to read - Tom Swift, the Tolkein books - but also to watch television, which I did plenty of lying on the carpet of our empty living room in the long dull afternoons after school.
>
> [...]My father was mean, and our house ugly, and my mother didn't pay much attention to me; my clothes were cheap and my haircut too short and no one at school seemed to like me that much; and since all this had been true for as long as I could remember, I felt things would doubtless continue in this depressing vein as far as I could foresee. In short: I felt my existence was **tainted**, in some **subtle** but essential way.
>
> **prone to** likely to have
> **circumstance** how things were
> **tainted** flawed, blemished
> **subtle** not immediately obvious

✏ Activity 1   Understanding the text

a) What specific objects does the narrator remember best from his childhood?

------

b) What kind of student was he at school?

------

c) Circle the meaning of the word 'vein' in this context:

    a blood vessel   a pathway

d) The narrator describes his childhood as 'depressing'. Pick out four facts that support this description.

Colons and semi-colons in context   5

✏️ Activity 2   Exploring the writer's technique

a) In the first sentence, the writer uses a colon and semi-colons. What does the colon do here and what do the semi-colons do?

----

b) Look again at the sentence beginning, 'I did well in school....' Here the semi-colon links two closely related points. Explain how they are linked.

----

c) The narrator sums up his feelings with the phrase 'In short' and follows this with a colon. Circle what you think the colon is helping to do:

- introduce a list
- introduce an example
- introduce an explanation
- introduce a quotation

d) Why does the writer use a colon instead of a comma after 'In short'? Think about the effect it has on the reader.

> **Tip**
>
> Think about how a colon often introduces things, but a semi-colon links things that are equally important, or contrasting.

✏️ Activity 3   Try it yourself

On a separate piece of paper, write a short description of something you remember from your childhood. Make sure that it includes:

- semi-colons to separate longer items in a list
- a semi-colon to link two closely related clauses
- a colon to introduce an explanation.

Use the extract opposite as a model for your writing. You could begin like this:

When I remember my childhood, I can easily recall my favourite toys:

69

Punctuation

6 Lists

What are lists?

A list is a number of items recorded one after the other. They can be presented in different ways; for example, a list can be laid out as one item per line (like a shopping list) or it can be laid out as part of a paragraph.

How does it work?

Punctuation can be very important in a list, either to introduce the items or to help separate out detailed items into clear chunks in order to avoid confusion. Colons, commas and semi-colons have an important part to play.

Colons and commas

Colons have a variety of uses but one of the most common is to introduce lists.

> Please go and buy**:** sugar**,** eggs**,** flour**,** nails**,** light bulbs**,** chewing gum **and** food for the pet gorilla.

colon → *commas* → *conjunction*

The items in the list above are separated from each other by a comma, apart from the final item, which follows the word 'and'. Notice that there is no comma before the 'and'.

Semi-colons

In a list of short, simple items, commas can be used to separate the items. However, if the items are longer, for example if they are clauses or contain a lot of detail, it is sometimes clearer to use semi-colons.

> To build a wolf-proof house, each lamb must ensure that: he uses bricks**;** the mortar is based on lime and gravel**;** he doesn't employ unreliable builders**;** he digs strong foundations and he fits video surveillance cameras.

semi-colons used to separate clauses in the list

Find out more

See page 66 for more about colons and page 64 for more about the Oxford comma.

Tip

In some lists, the word before the final item is a conjunction, such as 'and' or 'or'.

Shopping list
sugar
eggs
flour
nails
light bulbs
chewing gum
gorilla food

Lists 6

Activity 1

Add the correct punctuation to the lists below. The first one has been done for you.

a) I will not have these people in the house: Max, Ying, Megan, Jamie, Nimish or Ethan.

b) Make sure that you have laid out the following items a pen a pencil a ruler a protractor and a cup of coffee

c) Please remember to buy emulsion paint paintbrushes white spirit wallpaper wallpaper paste nails cloths and a bottle of juice

d) I have had many names Barack Tom William Zuka and Matthew

e) The principal would not tolerate the following talking grinning loud breathing eye-rolling swearing or horrible music at school

/4

Activity 2

Read the following statements carefully and tick whether they are true or false.

Statement	True	False
a) A list can be introduced with a semi-colon.		
b) Short items in a list are usually separated with semi-colons.		
c) Detailed, longer items in a list can be separated by semi-colons.		
d) A list can be introduced with a colon.		

/4

Activity 3

Add suitable punctuation to the lists below.

a) Go away and don't come back until you have found the Golden Fleece the meaning of life the secret of eternal youth or the potion of immortality

b) You are forbidden to drink the bottle labelled 'Drink Me' to eat the biscuits marked 'Eat me' to open the locked door or to cry at any time during this adventure

c) Students who enrol for this trip will need to bring sleeping bags a cloth or plastic rucksack a good supply of wands a book of protection spells and a flask of hot cocoa

d) I think that your son is extremely handsome devastatingly intelligent wonderfully talented in all science subjects a superb actor a fine singer and a suitable husband for my daughter

/4

Punctuation

7 Apostrophes for possession

What are apostrophes for possession?

An apostrophe is a punctuation mark that looks like a comma (or a small tadpole) suspended in mid-air.

An apostrophe can show that one thing belongs to another thing or person. This type of apostrophe is called a 'possessive apostrophe'.

How does it work?

Singular nouns

To show possession in a formal way, we could write or say:

The wisdom of the **owl** — possessing noun

The wisdom belongs to the owl, so the owl is the possessing noun.

However, it is more natural to write or say:

The owl's wisdom — apostrophe shows that the wisdom belongs to the owl

Here, the apostrophe goes after the possessing noun, and before the 's'.

Plural nouns

When the possessing noun is a plural, the apostrophe goes after the final letter (which is often, but not always, 's').

The crews of the **starships** — possessing noun

The starships' crews — apostrophe shows that the starships belong to the crews

If the plural noun does not end in an **–s** or **–es**, the apostrophe still goes after the final letter of the word and before a final 's'.

The deviousness of the **children** — possessing noun

The children's deviousness — apostrophe shows that the deviousness belonged to all the children

> **Tip**
> Remember that 'singular' means just one, and 'plural' means more than one. Plurals often end in **–s** or **–es**, but not always.

> **Tip**
> Apostrophes are **never** used to make plurals!
>
> Juicy pineapple's 70p a kilo ✗
>
> Juicy pineapples 70p a kilo ✓

Apostrophes for possession — 7

Activity 1

Underline the possessing noun in each of the following phrases and add the apostrophe in the correct place.

a) That dinosaurs tomato sandwiches

b) A womans determination

c) A tortoises speed record

d) Stephens homegrown strawberries

e) Aryas book of poetry

f) This warriors slippers

/6

Activity 2

Rewrite the following phrases into the usual shorter form and add an apostrophe to show possession. The first one has been done for you.

a) The hats of the camel   The camel's hats.

b) The hats of the camels ⁃⁃⁃⁃⁃⁃⁃⁃⁃⁃⁃⁃⁃⁃⁃⁃⁃⁃⁃⁃⁃⁃⁃⁃⁃⁃⁃⁃⁃⁃

c) The food of the baby ⁃⁃⁃⁃⁃⁃⁃⁃⁃⁃⁃⁃⁃⁃⁃⁃⁃⁃⁃⁃⁃⁃⁃⁃⁃⁃⁃⁃⁃⁃

d) The food of the babies ⁃⁃⁃⁃⁃⁃⁃⁃⁃⁃⁃⁃⁃⁃⁃⁃⁃⁃⁃⁃⁃⁃⁃⁃⁃⁃⁃⁃⁃⁃

e) The lair of the children ⁃⁃⁃⁃⁃⁃⁃⁃⁃⁃⁃⁃⁃⁃⁃⁃⁃⁃⁃⁃⁃⁃⁃⁃⁃⁃⁃⁃⁃⁃

f) The fillings of the teeth ⁃⁃⁃⁃⁃⁃⁃⁃⁃⁃⁃⁃⁃⁃⁃⁃⁃⁃⁃⁃⁃⁃⁃⁃⁃⁃⁃⁃⁃⁃

g) The dreadlocks of Polly ⁃⁃⁃⁃⁃⁃⁃⁃⁃⁃⁃⁃⁃⁃⁃⁃⁃⁃⁃⁃⁃⁃⁃⁃⁃⁃⁃⁃⁃⁃

/6

Activity 3

All the sentences below need apostrophes to show that one thing possesses another thing. Put one apostrophe into the right place in each sentence.

a) One monkey stole the other monkeys xylophone.

b) Two pandas oath of revenge.

c) The fairys wings were broken.

d) Dad knocked over the babys milk and Mum told him off.

e) Mum knocked over both babies bottles and they started crying.

f) Both dragons headaches were worsened by the noise of battle.

/6

Punctuation

8 Apostrophes for contraction

What are apostrophes for contraction?

An apostrophe is used to show that some letters are missing when two words are combined and shortened (contracted).

How does it work?

An apostrophe acts like a place marker in the contracted words. They mark where one or more of the letters has been taken out.

do not ⟶ **don't**

Notice how the two words are pushed together and the apostrophe marks the missing 'o'.

Some other commonly contracted words are:

We have had three weeks.	⟶	**We've** had three weeks.
He has caught a fish.	⟶	**He's** caught a fish.
I will come too.	⟶	**I'll** come too.
They had all been eaten.	⟶	**They'd** all been eaten.
We are all thrilled.	⟶	**We're** all thrilled.
She is not pretending anymore.	⟶	**She's** not pretending anymore.
He would do anything for you.	⟶	**He'd** do anything for you.

It is easy to confuse 'its' and 'it's'. Remember that **it's** is a contraction for '**it is**' or '**it has**'.

When you are writing a sentence and you aren't sure whether to add an apostrophe, check if the sentence would make sense if the words were written out in full. If they would, then you need to include an apostrophe.

It's three times heavier than me. — 'It is' still makes sense in this sentence, so it is a contraction.

Its tail had spikes. — 'It is tail had spikes' doesn't make sense, so it isn't a contraction.

Apostrophes for contraction 8

Activity 1

a) Write the contractions below out in full. The first one has been done for you. Note that some contractions may have two full versions.

  i. we've — we have
  ii. Josh's — ....
  iii. they're — ....
  iv. don't — ....
  v. I'll — ....

b) Write the contractions for the words below.

  i. he had — ....
  ii. it is — ....
  iii. would have — ....
  iv. who is — ....
  v. she will — ....

Tip
Beware of confusing **who's** (a contraction for 'who is' or 'who has') with **whose** (a pronoun meaning 'of whom' or 'of which').

/9

Activity 2

Read the sentences below. Circle the words that could be contracted and then write the contractions, using an apostrophe in the correct place. The first one has been done for you.

a) (She has) gone out and (you will) have to follow her. — She's, you'll
b) You have got to climb to the top of the mountain. — ....
c) They are bursting to tell you their news. — ....
d) You should not have done that; it will make her unhappy. — ....
e) That is not a very kind thing to say, is it? — ....

/5

Activity 3

Cross out the incorrect word in each sentence below.

a) **Whose / Who's** left the butter out of the fridge?
b) As for that film, **it's / its** such a bore.
c) **Who's / Whose** coffee is this?
d) The meerkat scampered back to **its / it's** burrow.
e) **Who's / Whose** your favourite doctor?
f) **Its / It's** about time you learned some respect, young man.

/6

75

Punctuation

9 Direct speech

What is direct speech?

Direct speech is the exact words that someone says.

> "**I have some fantastic news for you**," said the sports coach.

How does it work?

Direct speech uses speech marks (also known as inverted commas) to mark the beginning and end of the words spoken.

> "I have to tell you, Prime Minister, that you have lost the election."

Tip

Think of 66 for the first set of speech marks and 99 for the second set.

Direct speech always begins with a capital and is punctuated within the speech marks. This means that the comma, full stop, exclamation mark or question mark that a sentence needs has to come **before** the second set of speech marks.

> "You're not going out dressed like that, are you**?**" she laughed.

Sometimes the speaker is referred to in the middle of the speech. In this case, a comma is used twice.

> "Will you please explain**,**" Mum asked**,** "why you haven't dusted the stairwell?"

comma before closing of speech marks

comma before next set of speech marks

If the speaker is referred to before the speech, a comma or a colon can be used.

> She put down the essay and said**:** "That is the best work I've read."
>
> She put down the essay and said**,** "That is the best work I've read."

When punctuating a conversation, always start a new line for each new speaker.

> King Arthur gazed in satisfaction at the castle.
>
> "Camelot! At last," he breathed.
>
> "Yes, my liege," echoed Sir Bedevere. "Camelot!"
>
> "It's only a bit of CGI and green screen," mumbled Morgaine. "Don't get so excited."

Tip

There are many more interesting words to use than 'said'. For example: exclaimed, groaned, yelled, cried, muttered, whispered, growled, shouted or shrieked.

Direct speech 9

Activity 1

Add the correct punctuation to the direct speech in each example below.

a) She said Twenty dollars isn't enough for your night out so take forty.

b) You can borrow my fishing tackle if you like he muttered.

c) I've told you before not to talk while you're eating she growled.

d) Is it about time that we closed the shop he asked.

/4

Activity 2

Rewrite the sentences below, putting the speaker in the middle and changing the punctuation appropriately. The first one has been done for you.

a) "She's read your website and she actually likes it," he said.

"She's read your website," he said, "and she actually likes it."

b) "If I ruled the world, there would be free ice cream for everyone," he said.

----

c) "When I ask you to tidy your room, I don't like you rolling your eyes at me," she said.

----

d) "This isn't a day for working. This is a day for lying in the sun," he said.

/3

Activity 3

Read the conversation below and add the correct punctuation.

I've had a terrible day Yara said

What's the trouble Will asked I hope I can help

It's one of the girls she moaned Susan Jefferson

Oh dear She's your problem too he murmured

Susan knows more science than I'll ever know Yara sighed She's a genius

So your problem is that you feel you should resign and let her take over he joked

Not quite Yara groaned But she has built a time machine in my lab

/7

77

Punctuation

Direct speech in context

Extract from an article 'I would have been in care if my big sister hadn't stepped in' by Louise Tickle, in *The Times Magazine,* Saturday, 21 April 2018

The following text is taken from an article about children who are looked after by extended family rather than by their parents. Here, the journalist talks to Massiah and his sister, Malaika, who cares for him.

At a nearby café, Massiah digs into an enormous slice of carrot cake, after checking with '**Laika**' that he can have it. "We have a very playful relationship, but he does know I'm the adult and he has to listen," she says. "We have a full routine. Monday, online maths, English and Portuguese. Tuesday, kickboxing. Wednesday, cook together.
5   Thursday, swimming. Friday, it changes. Saturday, football. Sunday, Sunday school."

What do you think about living with Laika, I ask Massiah.

"It's fun," he says. "She takes me to fun places." He smiles up at her. "Like the funfair."

"And he has to do chores," she teases.

"Yes, I do the washing-up. And hang up the clothes. And I clean the cat litter."

10   Do you ever miss your mummy, I ask.

"Yes," is his immediate answer.

Laika Malaika, Massiah's older sister and carer

✏ Activity 1 | Understanding the text

a) What does Massiah enjoy eating?

---

b) What does Massiah spend time doing on a Wednesday?

---

c) What chores does Massiah do?

---

d) Circle the correct meaning of the word 'litter' in this context:

rubbish   to scatter about   an absorbent material used to collect pets' waste

e) How does Massiah feel about his mother?

Direct speech in context 9

✏️ Activity 2 Exploring the writer's technique

a) At the beginning of this text the writer does not start a new line when Malaika speaks. Why is this correct?

----

b) On two occasions the writer speaks directly to Massiah but does not use speech marks. Underline these two lines. Why do you think the writer does this and what effect does it have on the reader? Tick the answer that you agree with most:

☐ The reader knows this is an interview and so the speech marks are not needed.

☐ Only the interviewer's words are shown without speech marks and so the reader understands that these lines are her questions.

☐ Some writers now experiment with other ways of presenting speech and this may be what the journalist is doing.

c) Look again at the line, '"And he has to do chores," she teases'.

What does the word 'teases' help to convey here?

----

d) The writer uses the word 'says' twice.

   i. Circle an alternative for one of these from the following list:

   replies   states   grins   exclaims   explains

   ii. Explain which 'says' you would replace with the word you have circled and why.

✏️ Activity 3 Try it yourself

On a separate piece of paper, write down part of a conversation you can imagine having with a friend or family member about your weekly routine. Include correct speech punctuation and vary your vocabulary for the word 'said' or 'says'.

Spelling

1 Why is spelling important?

Learning to spell correctly is important because it helps to make your writing clear and it avoids confusion. It also makes your writing appear more confident. Your readers will focus more on what you say without being distracted by spelling errors. Future employers will expect you to be able to spell and, of course, marks for spelling are given in all English examinations.

Why is spelling so tricky in the English language?

There are 44 speech sounds in the English language, but only 26 letters. This means that we need to use different letter combinations to make different sounds. For example, we use the letters 's' and 'h' to make the sound 'sh', like at the end of the word ma**sh**.

The English language has evolved over hundreds of years, bringing changes in pronunciation and new words from other languages, such as **pyjamas** (from Urdu and Persian) and **poppadom** (from Tamil). English is still changing and new words are constantly being absorbed into the language.

Understanding how words are formed and looking at common letter patterns will help to improve your spelling. However, the 'rules' of English spellings are broken as often as they are followed, so some words just need to be learned in their own right. How you learn these will depend on what strategies work for you.

Find out more

See page 92 for more about different learning strategies for spellings.

✏ Activity 1

In the following words, circle the pairs of letters that make just one sound. One has been done for you.

(ph)oto   thud   shed   chips   mash   inch   sloth   Ophelia

/7

80

2 Vowels and consonants

What are vowels and consonants?

These letters are vowels: a, e, i, o u.

Vowels can make a short sound, such as the 'o' in n**o**t, or a long sound, such as the 'o' in h**o**me.

All the other letters are consonants: b c d f g h j k l m n p q r s t v w x y z.

Consonants usually only make one sound, like 'b' in **b**old. A few consonants can make more than one sound, such as c and g.

Say these words aloud and listen to the different sound made by the c and g:

| **c**risps | **c**eiling | **g**arlic | ra**g**ing |

Long vowel sounds

Some long vowel sounds can be spelled in many different ways.

The 'ay' sound, as in 'play', can also be spelled:

ai, as in r**ai**se   **a_e** as in sh**a**m**e**   **ey**, as in th**ey**   **ea**, as in br**ea**k   **a**, as in **a**corn

The 'e' sound, as in 'fee', can also be spelled:

ea, as in fl**ea**   **ey**, as in k**ey**   **ie**, as in th**ie**f   **e_e**, as in th**e**m**e**   **ei**, as in rec**ei**ve   **e**, as in m**e**

The 'i' sound, as in 'mind', can also be spelled:

igh, as in h**igh**   **ie**, as in p**ie**   **ui**, as in disg**ui**se   **i_e** as in t**i**d**e**   **y**, as in m**y**

The 'o' sound, as in 'go', can also be spelled:

oa, as in g**oa**t   **ow**, as in t**ow**ed   **eau**, as in chat**eau**   **ough**, as in d**ough**
oe, as in w**oe**   **o_e**, as in c**o**d**e**

Spelling

The 'oo' sound, as in 'zoo', can also be spelled:

ue, as in tr**ue**   **u_e**, as in r**u**d**e**   **ew**, as in gr**ew**   **o**, as in wh**o**
ou, as in y**ou**   **u**, as in r**u**thless   **ui**, as in s**ui**t

The 'yu' sound, as in 'cube', can also be spelled:

ue, as in arg**ue**   **ew**, as in kn**ew**   **eu**, as in f**eu**d
u, as in t**u**na

Tip

A 'silent e' is one that is not pronounced at the end of a word, but it can turn a short vowel sound into a long vowel sound. For example, **tap** into **tape**.

✏️ Activity 1

Write down two words that would fit for each sound. Circle the letters that make up the long vowel sounds in your words. The first one has been done for you.

a) the long 'ay' sound: c(a)k(e)
                          st(ay)

b) the long 'e' sound   _____
   _____

c) the long 'i' sound   _____
   _____

d) the long 'o' sound   _____
   _____

e) the long 'oo' sound   _____
   _____

f) the 'yu' sound   _____
   _____

Our living room is cr**ea**m with a h**u**ge family photo on the shelf.

/10

3 Plurals

What are plurals?

Plural means more than one. It is the opposite of singular, which means just one.

singular noun *plural noun*

One **hamster** is happy on its own but two **hamsters** may fight.

How are they formed?

Most plural nouns are made by adding **–s** to the singular noun.

creature + **s** = creature**s**

If the plural noun ends with an 'iz' sound, then it is spelled **–es**.

fox + **es** = fox**es**

If the noun ends in **–y**, we change the y into an i and add **–es**.
But if there is a vowel (a, e, i, o, u) before the y, just add an **s**.

family + i + es = famil**ies**   monkey + **s** = monkey**s**

Irregular plurals

Some plurals are irregular – they do not follow any rules – so they just need to be learned.

person ➔ people   tooth ➔ teeth   mouse ➔ mice   man ➔ men   woman ➔ women

Some other nouns are the same in the singular and plural such as 'fish' or 'deer'.

✏ Activity 1

In the following extract, the writer has made mistakes with all the plurals.
Write the corrections in the spaces provided. The first one has been
done for you.

The monkies <u>monkeys</u> were wondering how best to bring up their babys _____. Should they teach them to believe in fairys _____ or was that something that would only confuse monkey childs _____? It was hard enough getting them to be wary of human man's _____ and womans _____, who didn't always have good intentions towards creature's _____ like them. In the end, the monkey parent's _____ decided to leave it to the senior monkey's _____ to make the decision.

/8

83

Spelling

4 Silent letters

What are silent letters?

Some words contain silent letters, which we don't pronounce.

> **k**nife   **g**nat   **k**night   t**w**o   lam**b**

Why are they silent?

The reason that we have these silent letters in some words is because these letters used to be pronounced. For example, in the Middle Ages, when Geoffrey Chaucer was writing *The Canterbury Tales*, some words would have been pronounced differently.

> The word 'knife' would have sound like *ker-n-ee-f* (the 'k' could be heard).
>
> The word 'gnat' would have sounded like *ger-nat* (with a hard 'g').
>
> The word 'knight' would have sounded like *ker-nicht* (gh made a sound like the ch in the Scottish word, 'loch').
>
> The word 'two' was pronounced *ter-woe* (a bit like an owl!).

It is tricky to learn the spellings of words with silent letters. One strategy is to say the word aloud, sounding out all the letters, as they used to do in the Middle Ages. This might also help you learn the spellings of words that sound the same but have different spellings and different meanings. We call these words homophones.

Find out more

There is more about homophones on page 90.

As long as the whole word isn't made up of silent letters!

Silent letters 4

✏️ Activity 1

Circle the silent letters in the words below.

gnat   doubt   castle   dumb   design   scissors

knee   know   receipt   write

/10

✏️ Activity 2

All the words below are missing their silent letters. Rewrite them in their complete form in a sentence below. The first one has been done for you.

a) num — The cold weather was making my fingers numb.

b) nowledge

c) autum

d) rench

e) fasinate

f) nack

g) musle

h) whisle

i) condem

j) rist

/9

Spelling

5 Prefixes

What are prefixes?

A prefix is a group of letters that can be added before the root (basic) form of a word to make a new word. 'Pre' means 'before'.

prefix → un + necessary = unnecessary ← root word

Prefixes rarely change their spelling, although they can be added to different root words. They do not change the spelling of the root word either. They just add to it.

Common prefixes

Some common prefixes are listed below.

Prefix	Meaning	Example
un	not / the opposite of	unexpected
dis	not	disapprove
super	above / over / beyond	superman
sub	under	submarine
auto	on its own	autobiography
mono	one	monotone
bi	two	bicycle
tri	three	triangle

Activity 1

Draw a line to match a prefix with a suitable root word. Write out the new word and a definition for each one. The first one has been done for you.

Prefix	Root word	New word	Definition
a) un	appear	disappear	cease to be visible
b) dis	graph		
c) mono	usual		
d) super	heading		
e) sub	focal		
f) bi	chrome		
g) auto	hero		

/12

86

6 Suffixes

What are suffixes?

A suffix is a group of letters that can be added to the end of the root (basic) form of a word.

root word → **mend** + **ed** = mended ← suffix

Adding the suffix –ed to verbs

The suffix **–ed** is often added to the present tense of regular verbs to turn them into the past tense.

present tense → **confess** + ed = **confessed** ← past tense

If a regular verb ends in an e in the present tense, it loses it before the suffix **–ed** is added to make the past tense.

rul~~e~~ + ed = ruled

Adding the suffix –ing to verbs

The suffix **–ing** is added to verbs to turn them into a form of the present tense. This form is also called the present continuous or present progressive tense, because it means that it is happening now and continuing to happen.

study + ing = studying   distract + ing = distracting

I love **studying** grammar.   Stop **distracting** those who want to work.

If the verb ends in an e, cross off the e before adding the suffix **–ing**:

rul~~e~~ + ing = ruling   decid~~e~~ + ing = deciding

Adding the suffix –ly to form adverbs

If you know how words are formed, it helps you to spell them correctly.

An adverb is usually created by adding **–ly** to an adjective.

feverish + ly = feverishly   joyful + ly = joyfully

However, if the adjective already ends in a y, we need to replace the y with an i and then add **–ly** to make the adverb.

cra~~z~~y + i + ly = crazily   speed~~y~~ + i + ly = speedily

Find out more

There is more about verb tenses on page 14.

Find out more

There is more about adverbs on page 28.

Spelling

Adjectives that end in **–le** drop the final e and add **–y** to make the adverb.

simpl~~e~~ + ly = simply   terribl~~e~~ + ly = terribly

Adjectives that end in **–ic** *usually* add **–ally** to make them into an adverb.

realistic + ally = realistically   tragic + ally = tragically

Some adverbs are spelled the same way as the adjective.

| adjective describing the paper | The **daily** paper was read **daily** by the old man. | adverb describing frequency |

Adding the suffix –ness to make nouns

Some adjectives can be turned into nouns by adding the suffix **–ness**.

sad + ness = sadness

fair + ness = fairness

However, if the adjective ends in y, we need to change the y into an i before adding **–ness**.

happy   happ~~y~~ + i + ness = happiness

lazy   laz~~y~~ + i + ness = laziness

Adding the suffix –er to verbs to make nouns

Some verbs can be turned into nouns by adding the suffix **–er**.

eat + er = eater   paint + er = painter

If the verb ends in a single vowel and single consonant, you need to double the consonant before adding the suffix.

run + n + er = runner   sit + t + er = sitter

Suffixes 6

Activity 1

Add the suffixes –ed (to make the past tense) and –ing (to make the present continuous tense) to these root verbs. Write out the new words in the spaces provided. Remember that the final e on some root verbs will need to be dropped.

Root word	Past tense	Present continuous
a) rain		
b) pollute		
c) tangle		
d) work		

/8

Activity 2

Turn the adjectives below into adverbs. The first one has been done for you.

a) quiet   quietly

b) lazy   _____

c) beautiful   _____

d) horrible   _____

/3

Activity 3

Turn the following words into nouns by adding either –ness or –er.
The first one has been done for you.

a) whistle   whistler

b) healthy   _____

c) jump   _____

d) mad   _____

e) listen   _____

f) shop   _____

g) glad   _____

/6

Spelling

7 Commonly confused words

Some words sound very similar in the English language and this can lead to common spelling or grammatical errors.

Of and have

The words 'of' and 'have' are often confused, particularly when we use the contracted form of 'have', which is ''ve'.

The word 'of' is a preposition.   The word 'have' is a verb.

> The return **of** the Queen   I will **have** ketchup, please.

Of and off

There is a slight difference in the pronunciation of these two words, but they are often confused.

The word 'off' can be an adverb, preposition, adjective or noun.

> Get your muddy shoes **off** my carpet. ✔
> Get your muddy shoes **of** my carpet. ✘

Woman and women

The singular and plural of these words are similar to 'man' and 'men'.

Singular	Plural
man	men
woman	women

One **woman** was a judge; the other two **women** were doctors.

singular

plural

Homophones

Words that sound the same but have different spellings and meanings are called homophones. For example, 'bored' and 'board' are homophones.

The word 'bored' means not interested. The word 'board' is a long flat piece of timber or stiff material.

Other common homophones are 'weather' and 'whether', and 'sea' and 'see'.

Find out more

There is more about prepositions on page 26, verbs on page 10, adjectives on page 6 and adverbs on page 28.

Commonly confused words 7

There, their, they're

The word 'there' indicates a place.

The word 'their' is a possessive determiner.

I am going over **there** to the bus stop.

Those are **their** jet skis.

The word 'they're' is a contraction of 'they are'.

They're very tired now so **they're** going to pack up.

To, too and two

The word 'two' is a number.

The word 'to' is a preposition.

We have **two** choices to make.

I love going **to** school.

The word 'too' is an adverb, and can mean more than is wanted, or also.

There is **too** much food on this plate.

May I come **too**?

Activity 1

Read the sentences below. They all contain commonly confused words. Tick the ones that are correct and cross the ones that are incorrect. The first one has been done for you.

a) She would **of** chosen a different robot if she hadn't been so rushed. ✗

b) Take **off** the lid and look inside. ☐

c) Three **woman** prophesy that Macbeth shall become king. ☐

/2

Activity 2

Circle the correct homophone in the sentences below. The first one has been done for you.

a) Those kids, **there** / **(they're)** very rude and they never listen!

b) I think you should camp over **their** / **there** in the swamp.

c) The trouble is, **they're** / **their** feet are swollen.

d) The **two** / **to** owls were **too** / **to** / **two** sleepy.

/4

Activity 3

Choose there/their/they're or to/two/too and on separate paper, write three sentences using each homophone correctly.

/3

91

8 How to learn spellings

Different learning strategies suit different people. Try out some of the strategies below to find one or two methods that suit you.

Mnemonics

A mnemonic is a verse or saying that helps you to remember something.

For example, if you struggle to remember the spelling of 'embarrassed', learn this saying:

> If you are emba**rr**a**ss**ed, you are **really red** and a **silly sausage** (double r, double s).

Here are some other mnemonics that some people find helpful.

- 'Separate' – has **A RAT** in it.
- 'Because' – **b**ig **e**lephants **c**an **a**lways **u**nderstand **s**mall **e**lephants.
- '**R**hythm' – **h**as **y**our **t**wo **h**ips **m**oving.

Drawings

Some people find drawings helpful when learning spellings.

> Necessary has **one collar** and **two sleeves** (one c and double s).

Highlight and repeat

There is often just one tricky part of a word to spell. If this is the case, write out the word and underline the part that you can't remember.

> beautiful

Then learn the highlighted letters by repeating them in a chant or writing them out many times.

How to learn spellings 8

Look-cover-write-check

Follow the steps below to memorise the spelling of tricky words.

- **Look** at the word and learn it using your favourite technique.
- **Cover** the word up.
- **Write** the word out.
- **Check** that you have spelled the word correctly.

If you haven't, then go through steps 1 to 4 again and repeat until you've learned the word.

Activity 1

Write down two words that you struggle to spell. Then make up a mnemonic to help you remember the tricky part of each spelling. It doesn't matter how silly it is, as long as it is memorable!

a) ....

b) ....

/2

Activity 2

On separate paper, write down another word that you find tricky to spell (nouns work particularly well with this strategy). Think carefully about the tricky part of the spelling and then draw a picture with a feature that will help you to remember it.

/6

Activity 3

Some commonly misspelled words are listed below. Try using some of these new ways of learning them, then test yourself.

Tip

Set yourself a target of learning five spellings per week. These could be from any subject, not just English.

Glossary

adjective a word that describes a person, place or object (nouns and pronouns)

adjective phrase a group of words that acts as an adjective and has an adjective as its headword

adverb a word that gives more detail about a verb, an adjective or another adverb

adverbs of frequency adverbs that say how often something happens, e.g. *sometimes* or *rarely*

adverbs of time adverbs that say when something is taking place, e.g. *tomorrow* or *later*

adverb phrase a group of words that acts as an adverb and has an adverb as its headword

apostrophe for contraction an apostrophe to show that some letters are missing when two words are combined and shortened (contracted), e.g. *don't* or *we're*

apostrophe for possession (or possessive apostrophe) an apostrophe that shows that one thing belongs to another thing or person, e.g. the boy's shoes

auxiliary verb a helping verb that comes before the main verb to help express a tense

capital letter an upper case letter, e.g. A, B or C. Lower case letters are smaller, e.g. a, b or c

clause a group of words that work together as a unit with a verb as its headword

colon a punctuation mark **:** that can be used to introduce a list, examples or explanations

comma a punctuation mark **,** used to separate information. It can separate items in a list, clauses or direct speech from information about the speaker

command a sentence that usually begins with a verb and instructs you to do something

common noun a noun that names a general thing rather than a particular one, e.g. *girl* or *car*

comparative adjective an adjective that compares two things, e.g. she is *happier* than him

complex sentence a sentence that contains one main clause and at least one subordinate clause. The clauses are joined together by subordinating conjunctions. A complex sentence is a type of multi-clause sentence.

compound sentence a sentence that is made up of two or more clauses that are equally important and joined together by a coordinating conjunction. A compound sentence is a type of multi-clause sentence.

conjunction (or connective) a linking word that joins words, phrases or clauses, e.g. *if*, *but* or *and*

consonant these letters are consonants: b c d f g h j k l m n p q r s t v w x y z

coordinating conjunction a conjunction that joins two parts of a sentence that are of equal weight (they are both full clauses), e.g. *and*, *yet* or *for*

demonstrative determiner a determiner that shows (demonstrates) which item is meant by saying whether it is near or far, e.g. *this* bag or *those* apples

determiner a word that comes before a noun and gives more information about it, such as which one it is, how many there are, where it is and whose it is, e.g. *an*, *that* or *some*

dialogue spoken words between two or more people

direct speech the exact words that someone says. Direct speech uses speech marks (or inverted commas) to mark the beginning and end of the words spoken.

exclamation a sentence that expresses emotion such as surprise, enthusiasm or horror

exclamation mark a punctuation mark **!** that is usually placed at the end of a sentence to indicate that the sentence is an exclamation

full stop a punctuation mark **.** used to indicate the end of a sentence, or to show that a word has been shortened or abbreviated

future tense a tense used to describe things that will happen in the future

headword the most important word in a phrase

homophones words that sound the same but have different spellings and meanings, e.g. *bored* and *board*

indirect object a second object in a sentence that is directly affected after the main object

intensifying adverb an adverb that emphasises another adjective or adverb, e.g. *very* slowly or *really* exciting

irregular plural noun a plural noun that does not follow any spelling rules and just needs to be learned, e.g. *men* or *mice*

irregular verb a verb that changes in a unique way, not following the usual pattern and often changing the root of the word

list a number of items recorded one after the other

lower case letters smaller letters, e.g. a, b or c. Upper case (capital) letters are larger, e.g. A, B or C

Glossary

main clause a clause that contains a subject and verb, and makes sense on its own

main verb the main verb details the main action, state or feeling

mnemonic a verse or saying that helps to remember something

multi-clause sentence a sentence made up of more than one clause, each with its own verb; they can include two main clauses, or one main clause and one subordinate clause

noun a word used to name a person, place, idea or thing

noun phrase a group of words that acts as a noun and has a noun as its headword

object the object in a sentence is the person, animal or thing that is on the receiving end of the action (having something done to it)

paragraph a sentence or group of sentences on one idea that forms a distinct section in a piece of writing

past tense a tense used to describe things that have already happened

personal pronoun a word that can be used instead of a noun that refers to a person, people or things, e.g. *she, it, his*

phrase a group of words that form a unit; most phrases do not have a verb so they are not full sentences

plural more than one. It is the opposite of singular, which means just one

plural noun a noun that is more than one. Most plural nouns are made by adding –s or –es to the singular noun, e.g. *foxes* or *hats*

possessive determiner a determiner that shows ownership, e.g. *my, your, Jason's*

possessive pronoun a pronoun that refers to things that are owned, e.g. *mine, yours* or *his*

prefix a group of letters placed in front of a root word to add to or change its meaning, e.g. un– or dis–

preposition a word that comes before a noun, pronoun or noun phrase and links it to other words in the sentence. Prepositions tell you about position, direction, timing or another type of link or relationship

prepositional phrase a group of words that acts as a preposition and has a preposition as its headword

present tense a tense used to describe things that are happening now

pronoun a word that can be used instead of a noun

proper noun a noun that names a particular person, place or thing, e.g. *London, the Queen*

punctuation the marks, such as full stop or comma, used in writing to separate sentences and their parts, and to make meaning clear

quantifying determiner a determiner that details quantity or number, e.g. *all, many, fewer*

question a sentence that asks something

question mark a punctuation mark **?** that is usually placed at the end of a sentence to indicate that the sentence is a question

regular verb a verb that follows a set pattern, adding different endings, but leaving the root of the word unchanged

root a word in its most basic form, e.g. *look*

semi-colon a punctuation mark **;** that links together two main clauses that are of equal importance but that suggest a contrast or are closely related

sentence a group of words that expresses a complete idea. Sentences usually have a verb and form a statement, question, command or exclamation

silent letter a letter in a word that is not pronounced, e.g. **g** in **g**nat or **k** in **k**night

single-clause sentence a sentence comprised of one main clause. It is also known as a simple sentence.

singular just one. It is the opposite of plural, which means more than one

speech marks (or inverted commas) a punctuation mark that goes at the beginning **"** and end **"** of spoken words

statement a sentence that tells you something

subject the person, animal or thing in a sentence that is doing or being the verb

subordinate clause a clause that adds information to a main clause but can't work as a sentence on its own

subordinating conjunction these join a less important part of a sentence (subordinate clause) to the most important part of the sentence (main clause), e.g. *because, until, whereas*

suffix a group of letters that can be added to the end of the root form of a word, e.g –ed or –ing

superlative adjective an adjective that compares more than two things, e.g. she is happier than him, but the cat is *happiest* of all

upper case letters (or capital letters) larger letters, e.g. A, B or C. Lower case letters are smaller, e.g. a, b or c

verb a word that identifies actions, thoughts, feelings or a state of being

verb tense the three main verb tenses are past tense, present tense and future tense; they explain whether something is happening now, has already happened, or will happen in the future

vowel these letters are vowels: a, e, i, o u

OXFORD
UNIVERSITY PRESS

Great Clarendon Street, Oxford, OX2 6DP, United Kingdom

Oxford University Press is a department of the University of Oxford. It furthers the University's objective of excellence in research, scholarship, and education by publishing worldwide. Oxford is a registered trade mark of Oxford University Press in the UK and in certain other countries

Copyright © Oxford University Press 2019

The moral rights of the authors have been asserted.

First published in 2019

All rights reserved. No part of this publication may be reproduced, stored in a retrieval system, or transmitted, in any form or by any means, without the prior permission in writing of Oxford University Press, or as expressly permitted by law, by licence or under terms agreed with the appropriate reprographics rights organization. Enquiries concerning reproduction outside the scope of the above should be sent to the Rights Department, Oxford University Press, at the address above.

You must not circulate this work in any other form and you must impose this same condition on any acquirer

British Library Cataloguing in Publication Data

Data available

ISBN 978-019-842153-5

11

Printed and bound in Great Britain by Bell and Bain Ltd, Glasgow

The manufacturer's authorised representative in the EU for product safety is Oxford University Press España S.A. of El Parque Empresarial San Fernando de Henares, Avenida de Castilla, 2 – 28830 Madrid (www.oup.es/en or product.safety@oup.com). OUP España S.A. also acts as importer into Spain of products made by the manufacturer.

Acknowledgements

The authors and publisher are grateful for permission to include extracts from the following copyright material:

John Harding: *One Big Damn Puzzler* (Doubleday, 2005), copyright © John Harding 2005, reprinted by permission of The Random House Group Ltd.

Emma Hooper: *Etta and Otto and Russell and James* (Fig Tree Books, 2015), copyright © Emma Hooper 2015, reprinted by permission of Penguin Books Ltd.

John Harris: 'Save our children from the horrors of school sport', *The Independent*, 1 March 2000, reprinted by permission of the author.

Matthew Polly: *American Shaolin: Flying Kicks, Buddhist Monks, and the Legend of Iron Crotch* (Abacus, 2007), copyright © Matthew Polly 2007, reprinted by permission of the publishers, Little, Brown Book Group Ltd.

Meg Rosoff: *What I Was* (Penguin, 2008), copyright © Meg Rosoff 2008, reprinted by permission of Penguin Books Ltd.

Donna Tartt: *The Secret History* (Penguin, 2006/Viking 1992), copyright © Donna Tart 1992, reprinted by permission of Penguin Books Ltd and Alfred A Knopf, an imprint of the Knopf Doubleday Publishing Group, a division of Random House LLC.

Louise Tickle: 'I would have been in care if my big sister hadn't stepped in', *The Times Magazine*, 21 April 2018, copyright © Louise Tickle/ News UK & Ireland Ltd 2018, reprinted by permission of News Licensing.

The authors and publisher are grateful for permission to reprint the following copyright images:

Cover: MyImages – Micha/Shutterstock.

Illustrations by Oxford University Press.

We have tried to trace and contact all copyright holders before publication. If notified, the publishers will be pleased to rectify any errors or omissions at the earliest opportunity.